The
RECORDS
GUIDE
for the Family

The RECORDS GUIDE for the Family

by

WILLIAM F. KEEFE

J. G. FERGUSON PUBLISHING COMPANY

Chicago 1983

Library of Congress Cataloging in Publication Data

Keefe, William Ford, 1921-
The records guide for the family.

1. Family records. 2. Law—United States—Popular works. I. Title.
CS24.K43 1983 640 83-5603
ISBN 0-89434-035-2

G 6

Copyright © 1983 by J. G. Ferguson Publishing Company
All rights reserved
Printed in the United States of America

TABLE OF CONTENTS

1	**INTRODUCTION: THE LAW NEEDS HELP**

7	**PART I: WHAT IS A LAWYER AND WHAT DOES HE NEED?**
9	Checklist of Information for Your Lawyer
15	Family Identification Numbers That Your Lawyer May Need
17	Simplified Power of Attorney
18	Which Papers to Keep Where

19	**PART II: ON THE TRACK OF REAL PROPERTY**
21	Buying a Home? Here's What to Look For
24	Technical/Financial Questions to Consider When Buying a Home
26	A Sample Real Estate Contract of Sale
27	Papers That May be Needed When You Close Your Real Estate Sale
28	A Checklist on Sole and Joint Ownership of Property
29	**The Family Home: Your Complete Guide and Record**
30	Our Home
32	Home Improvements
33	Household Inventory
47	Household Inventory Summary
48	Appliances and Warranties
54	Other Personal Property
56	General Home Maintenance and Repairs
58	Property and Other Taxes

60	Home Office Expenses: Information for Calculating Deductibility
62	Your Home Security Checklist
63	Moving? Check Your Preparations Carefully
65	Vacation or Second Home Records
67	Real Estate Repairs—Vacation/Second Home

69 PART III: YOUR FAMILY HISTORY, BABY BOOK, INSURANCE, AND OTHER IMPORTANT MATTERS

71	**The View from the Family Tree**
72	Our Family Tree
73	Family Data Sheet
74	Oral History: Taping Golden Agers' Memories
76	Family Birth Information
77	Family Marriage Information
78	Children's Marriages
79	Adoption Records
81	Citizenship
83	Identification
84	Religious Affiliations
96	Activities—Community, Social, Religious, Other
102	Favorite Family Recipes
108	**Your Baby Book**
133	**Family Health: Your Complete Record**
134	Prenatal Care
136	Family Medical Background
138	Family Medical Background—Additional Information

139	Blood Group, Donations
145	Record of Blood Transfusions Received
146	The Newborn's Immunization Schedule
147	Immunizations: A Life Record
153	Adult Weight Record
159	Contagious Disease Records
183	Medical Alert—For Emergency and Reference Use
185	Health Examinations
187	Major Laboratory Examinations
189	Electrocardiograms
191	Hospital Admissions
195	Acute Illnesses
198	Accidents
200	Optical History
202	Dental History
204	X-Ray Histories
206	Prescribed Medications
208	Adverse Reactions to Prescribed Medications
210	Additional Health Records
212	**Until Death Us Do Part**
213	Wedding Gifts
216	Sample Apartment-Sharing Contract
217	Termination of Marriage Record
219	**Insurance: Health, Vehicle, Life, Homeowner's or Property, Mortgage, and Other Kinds**
220	Family and Individual Hospitalization and Health Insurance
224	Disability/Income Protection

225	Vehicle Insurance
227	Life Insurance
231	Third-Party Life Insurance
233	Homeowner's or Real Property Insurance
235	Mortgage Insurance
237	Endowment and Annuity Insurance
239	Personal Property Insurance
241	Other Policies
243	**Budgets and Other Concerns**
244	A Better Family Budget
249	The Budget Supplement: A Monthly Buying-for-less Guide
250	Savings Record: Passbook Savings Accounts
251	Savings Record: U.S. Savings Bonds
252	Savings Record: Certificates of Deposit
253	Savings Record: Other
254	A Family Money-Flow Table
255	Safe Deposit Box
257	Bank Accounts
259	Credit Cards and Charge Accounts
261	Check Cashing Cards
262	Other Licenses, Cards, Etc.
263	Passports
265	Union Memberships
267	Workmen's Compensation Claims
269	Loan History
271	Investments: Securities
273	Investments: Special

275	**Pension, Profit-Sharing, Taxes, Retirement Planning**
276	Things to Know about Your Pension Plan
278	The Retirement Plan—Form 1
279	The Retirement Plan—Form 2
280	Pension and Profit-Sharing Plan
282	Income Taxes
284	Investment Art, Jewelry, and Antiques
286	**Wills, Trusts, Estate Planning**
287	How to Estimate the Size of Your Estate
292	Net Worth—Annual Calculation
294	Form for a Simple Will
295	What Every Husband and Wife Should Know after Drawing Up Wills
298	Trust Funds
299	Gifts, Bequests, and Wills
301	Last Will and Testament Locator
305	The Estate Planning Team
307	Reportable Gifts and Donations
308	Current Creditors
309	Current Debtors
310	Trust Property Record
311	Other Investments
312	Rental Property
313	Motor Vehicles
314	**Nothing Is Certain...**
315	Last Rites Information
317	Information in the Event of Death

323	Checklist—Steps to Take After a Family Loss
324	Checklist for My Executor
330	Uniform Donor Card ("Anatomical Gift")

331 PART IV: YOUR MONEY, YOUR RESUME, GOING INTO BUSINESS, MISCELLANY

333	Shopping for a Bank? Ask (At Least) These Questions
334	The Resume: Some Things to Include
335	Employment History
339	Education
345	Business History
347	Memberships in Organizations—With Offices, Honors, Awards
349	Military Service
351	Sports, Outside Interests, Hobbies
357	Travel
359	A Checklist on Franchises
360	Your Car Again: Calculating Present-Car Costs Versus New-Car Costs
361	The Family Automobile: Your Investment in Transportation
362	Pet Record
364	An Aide-Memoire—Important Dates to Remember

370 NOTES

INTRODUCTION

THE LAW NEEDS HELP

THE LAW NEEDS HELP

The law needs help. *Your* help. It can't operate in a vacuum.

Picture the things that can and do occur. You have reached the age of 30 and you want to make out your first will and testament. You will want to have a ready reference sheet that will tell you what you have to know about your worldly goods. You might want to see a model will or trust instrument.

Or you are hailed into court to respond in an accident case. Your memory tells you that the other car slammed into you at 3 o'clock. Or was it 5 o'clock?

Or you have decided to beat recession, depression, and prosperity at a single stroke by establishing an ironclad budget . . . Or you hear conflicting reports about where to store your key personal or family documents, and of course don't want to make a mistake . . . Or you are buying real estate and want to have a record of the highlights of the transaction . . .

In each case you could have a legal, or law-related, interest in having records that you can refer to later.

In literally hundreds of other situations you could face the need for records, guidesheets, checklists, references, logs, daybooks, diaries, or annals. The records might or might not have financial or monetary implications. They might have no more than emotional or commemorative meaning.

They might only help you when you come to write your autobiography. Or donate your vital organs upon your death.

Doing either of those things, you come back within the purview of the law. Copyright. A donor's agreement.

You're Not a Number

At some future date, as some humorist has pointed out, each person entering the world may have a number stamped on his chest. The number will be all this depersonalized, dehumanized entity will need. He or she or it will use the number when buying groceries, registering for school, checking a book out of the library, enlisting in the army, or buying an airplane ticket.

You can wage war, starting today with this book, against dehumanization. Against the digits that seem to be taking control of all our lives. Against the prophets of an Orwellian future who would like nothing better than to Newspeak you into living like a prole.

You can keep a record of your life, of your family, of your births and moves and major purchases and your children's illnesses.

These events make you what you are. They make up the experience record that sets you apart, individualizes you, distinguishes you, helps you survive, teaches you to avoid mistakes, arms you against the day when you will want to look it up.

Looking It Up

The truest story of all concerns the man who couldn't look it up. He's in the last place any of us wants to be: his lawyer's office. Facing an emotionally draining experience, he hears the simplest of all questions: "What, exactly, were the circumstances under which you took out this loan?"

Or: "Didn't you make notes that would tell us exactly what you two agreed on when it came to property?"

Or: "I really can't do much for you unless you can give me some specifics about your holdings."

Think of this the next time you're in your doctor's office. "Has this child had rubella?" he asks. Or: "Mr. Doe, we have to work fairly quickly. Does your son have any medicinal allergies?"

None of us, being human, escapes the lot of humankind. Each of us has normal failings. We may act carelessly once, lose our tempers another time. Is there a man or woman who has not overlooked a bill at one time or another? Who hasn't spoken when silence would have been golden?

The other question is: why compound normal human failings by rendering ourselves incapable of reconstructing or reproducing an event that happened earlier—at least in skeletal form?

The Dotted Line

Dotted lines keep popping up, demanding attention. You buy a washer-dryer. You agree to take a new insurance policy. You pick up a registered or express package at the post office. You buy a car or a house. You change your name or lease an apartment or apply for a fellowship or rent a lawnmower or apply for Social Security or Medicare benefits.

Each time you sign your name you are probably entering into a contract. In many other situations that involve what might be called invisible dotted lines, you are also entering into contracts. But in these less formal cases you may not be required to sign.

Unless you are buying with a credit card, you would not sign for gasoline at the local station, or for bread at the local supermarket, or for your clothes at the nearby drycleaners. You probably don't need a record of these transactions.

Where you are signing for something important, you may want to have a record. The contract, after all, binds both you and someone else to a certain course of action or to a given relationship.

These major dotted lines nearly always have a significance that reaches far beyond the moment of signature. How often has a court of law been asked to rule in a case in which a person died intestate—without a will—and left only scattered documents and records?

"There is the person's valid signature," the court may say, "so the deceased did sell the North 40 to Neighbor Yardley. Case dismissed."

No one needs to beware of dotted lines. He or she should simply not ignore them if they represent significant steps. Where they do, a simple record of the details should be noted.

Think in Categories

Forms for keeping track of life and its high points may seem to come in bewildering varieties. Not entirely so.

Certainly they come as compilations of data that may be legally required or useful in the future. That, one might guess, represents a very important category. But there are others of equal or nearly equal importance.

All of them are represented in the following pages. They include these principal types of forms and records:

• Forms for reference and guidance such as those that show the typical contents of a will, trust, or contract of sale.

• How-to forms and checklists that enable you to save money, dispose of property, papers, or other goods wisely or in alternative ways help you to reduce life's problems and frictions. An example: a form showing how to list your total assets or total estate.

• Summary or classificational forms, such as that used to list bank accounts, that provide information on a number of facts of your life, all of which fall in a specific class.

• Record forms that store information that you may or will definitely need in the future. An example: the family medical history form.

• Family events forms that make it possible to maintain a file of information including, as desired, dates, weights, places, and other data on family members. An example: the family birth information form.

• Personal forms for you and perhaps others close to you. An example: the military record form.

The Family Book

At one time the Bible served as the repository of much of the information that seemed to be important to the family's members, either immediately or in the future. In the 1980s life has grown so complex that record-keeping has become a way of life. Whatever the individual's status, he or she needs a running chronicle of the facts and events that may have emotional, legal, economic, or other meaning.

This book seeks to answer the need for that perfect record book. It will not guarantee that you will be prepared for every contingency, that you will avoid every snare, or that you will win every court case that involves you.

The book will, however, prepare you for most contingencies. It will also give you a tool for early detection of fine-print or large-print traps and give you information that you may need to take to court and defend or explain yourself.

The book may save you money. It includes some "how-to-buy-it-or-estimate-it" informational forms. If you have to hire legal counsel, the book will enable you to talk intelligently about your problems.

The Memory Book-Plus

This book, in brief, is a memory book, a Family Record Book, a legal aid, and a handy reference book. It should be kept, like any much used book, where you can refer to it readily and make notations in it quickly. Keep it safe but accessible.

Make notations in it? Yes. It has been designed to be used, to be written in, to be read. This book should become a treasury of indispensable information.

PART I

WHAT IS A LAWYER AND WHAT DOES HE NEED?

WHAT IS A LAWYER AND WHAT DOES HE NEED?

While you live, your life-agenda constitutes an unfinished record. Later it becomes a closed but still critically important set of facts.

If you are like nearly all of those who travel through life with you, you will at some point come into direct contact with the law. You will go looking for a lawyer and you may find yourself facing a judge.

If you are like every one of your contemporaries, you will be coming into indirect contact with the law just about every day of your life.

If you need a lawyer, or think you need a lawyer, it just might be useful to run your finger down a checklist, make a few marks, and establish in advance some of the things your lawyer may need to know. The checklist gives you quick answers and saves everyone's time (and your money). You may need to produce some basic documents (marriage license, lease contract, and so on) quickly.

A power of attorney may become necessary at one time or another. It gives your attorney or some other person the right to act for you in specific circumstances or a given situation that should be carefully described.

Some key forms for these purposes appear in Part I.

CHECKLIST OF INFORMATION FOR YOUR LAWYER

1. Names, addresses, ages, and other pertinent information of all parties:

___ a. Your name, address, phone number, age:

   Name _____

   Address _____

   City/State/Zip _____

   Home Phone _____ Office Phone _____ Age _____

___ b. Your spouse's name, address, phone number, age:

   Name _____

   Address _____

   City/State/Zip _____

   Home Phone _____ Office Phone _____ Age _____

___ c. The other parties:

   Name _____

   Address _____

   City/State/Zip _____

   Home Phone _____ Office Phone _____ Age _____

   Name _____

   Address _____

   City/State/Zip _____

   Home Phone _____ Office Phone _____ Age _____

   Name _____

   Address _____

   City/State/Zip _____

   Home Phone _____ Office Phone _____ Age _____

___ d. Witnesses:

   Name _____

   Address _____

CHECKLIST OF INFORMATION FOR YOUR LAWYER (cont'd)

City/State/Zip _____

Home Phone _____ Office Phone _____ Age _____

Name _____

Address _____

City/State/Zip _____

Home Phone _____ Office Phone _____ Age _____

Name _____

Address _____

City/State/Zip _____

Home Phone _____ Office Phone _____ Age _____

2. Details and facts relating to the matter:

   If accident:

   __ a. Date and time _____

   __ b. Location _____
   _____

   __ c. Description

   Personal injuries: _____
   _____
   _____

   Property damage: _____
   _____
   _____

   __ d. Physicians/hospitals/ambulance
   _____
   _____
   _____

   __ e. Auto registration _____

CHECKLIST OF INFORMATION
FOR YOUR LAWYER (cont'd)

___ f. Expenses incurred (medical, repairs, wages)

_____
_____
_____
_____

___ g. Employment (time lost) _____

___ h. Police officers

_____
_____
_____

___ i. Insurance company _____

_____

If matrimonial matter:

___ a. Maiden name _____

___ b. Date of marriage _____

___ c. Place of marriage _____

___ d. Names and birth dates of children

     Name _____ Date _____

     Name _____ Date _____

     Name _____ Date _____

     Name _____ Date _____

___ e. How long at present residence _____

___ f. Date and place of birth _____

___ g. Cause of marital breakup (dates and place of events complained of)

_____
_____
_____
_____

CHECKLIST OF INFORMATION FOR YOUR LAWYER (cont'd)

If house closing:

___ a. Address of house (description if possible)

_____

_____

_____

___ b. Old deed _____

___ c. Mortgage information

_____

_____

___ d. Purchase price _____

___ e. Terms _____

___ f. All personal property included in sale

_____

_____

_____

___ g. Closing date _____

For will or estate plan:

___ a. Name and address of all relatives who would be entitled to inherit if no will existed

Name _____

Address _____

Name _____

Address _____

Name _____

Address _____

Name _____

Address _____

CHECKLIST OF INFORMATION
FOR YOUR LAWYER (cont'd)

___ b. Complete list of all assets, including bank accounts, stocks, bonds, real estate, personal effects, household furnishings, mortgages, patents, etc.

Bank accounts _____

_____

Stocks _____

_____

_____

_____

Bonds _____

_____

_____

Real estate _____

_____

_____

Personal effects _____

_____

_____

Household furnishings _____

_____

_____

_____

Mortgages _____

_____

Patents _____

Misc. _____

CHECKLIST OF INFORMATION FOR YOUR LAWYER (cont'd)

___ c. In whose name assets are listed
_____

___ d. Life insurance

Company _____ Policy no. _____

Company _____ Policy no. _____

Company _____ Policy no. _____

___ e. Business interests
_____
_____
_____

___ f. Pension, profit sharing, death benefits
_____
_____

___ g. How you want estate distributed
_____
_____
_____
_____

___ h. When do you want minors to receive their inheritance
_____

___ i. Name and address of executor and guardian for infant children

Executor _____
_____

Guardian _____
_____

FAMILY IDENTIFICATION NUMBERS
THAT YOUR LAWYER MAY NEED

Family Member	Type of Identification	Number	Expires

FAMILY IDENTIFICATION NUMBERS
THAT YOUR LAWYER MAY NEED

Family Member	Type of Identification	Number	Expires

SIMPLIFIED POWER OF ATTORNEY

KNOW ALL MEN BY THESE PRESENTS:

I, _____, residing at
_____ ,
hereby make, constitute, and appoint _____
my true and lawful attorney in fact for and in my name, place, and stead, to _____
_____
_____
_____
_____ .

I grant and give to _____ in fact full authority and power to do and perform any and all acts necessary or incident to the performance and execution of the powers expressly granted herein as fully to all intents and purposes as I might or could do if personally present.

In witness whereof, I have hereunto signed my name this ____ day of _____, 19__.

_____
Signature

State of _____:

:ss.;

County of _____:

On the ____ day of _____, 19__, before me personally came _____ _____, to me known and known to me to be the individual described in, and who executed, the foregoing instrument, and (s)he acknowledged to me that (s)he executed the same.

_____
NOTARY PUBLIC

WHICH PAPERS TO KEEP WHERE

	Home Strongbox	Safe Deposit Box	Where Yours Is	As of (Date)
Apartment lease	✓			
Appraisals of jewelry, furs		✓		
Automobile titles		✓		
Birth certificates		✓		
Canceled checks	✓			
Charitable contribution records	✓			
Credit card numbers	✓			
Discharge papers		✓		
Equipment, appliance records	✓			
Government bonds		✓		
Home-improvement records	✓			
Income tax records	✓			
Insurance policies	✓			
Marriage certificate		✓		
Medical records	✓			
Mortgage		✓		
Payroll check stubs	✓			
Receipts	✓			
Savings passbooks	✓			
School records	✓			
Social Security records	✓			
Stock certificates		✓		
Wills	✓			
Wills (duplicate)		✓		
This book				

PART II

ON THE TRACK OF REAL PROPERTY

ON THE TRACK OF REAL PROPERTY

Because American law is largely derived from the English system of law, we take some things for granted. Among them, private ownership of property ranks high. So do the respective rights of tenant and landlord, the governmental right of condemnation or eminent domain, and easements. So do mortgages, quitclaim deeds, plats.

Private ownership of property has so many implications that they are difficult to count. The king, or the state, no longer owns all real property, and thus cannot demand services in return for the right of occupation. Taxes must be paid, of course. But land tenure need not be life-long, as it was under the feudal system. Each individual can own, buy, and sell land.

Equally importantly, a landlord or landowner can enter into a legal relationship that gives another person or persons the right to use or occupy. The owner becomes the landlord while the person leasing becomes the tenant.

The law applies directly where land is purchased, where landlord-lessor relationships occur, or where some other change takes place that affects the ownership or use of land, buildings, or other items of real or personal property. For that reason, records of key transactions are especially valuable.

Another reason might be cited. Where real estate is involved, the law becomes a jealous guardian of rights and interests. Years may pass; the law may continue in pursuit of a just decision in a case involving real estate.

There's a third reason for paying special attention to your records on the whole process of exchanging or leasing real estate: buying a piece of real estate may be the biggest single investment you will make in your lifetime.

Only slightly less important are the other types of real estate and personal or home property transactions.

In this section appear the record forms for how-to, what-occurred, what-you-have-to-know, and other types.

BUYING A HOME?
HERE'S WHAT TO LOOK FOR

Bathrooms	Yes	No	Adequate
Are there enough?	___	___	___
Are the tiling and caulking in good condition?	___	___	___
Are water pressure and drainage in the sink and tub sufficient?	___	___	___
Flush the toilet; does it sound cheap?	___	___	___
Or is the toilet relatively silent and smooth-running?	___	___	___
Are there trademarks on all the fixtures? If not, they may be second rate.	___	___	___
Are there sufficient electrical outlets?	___	___	___
Do the electrical outlets work?	___	___	___

Bedrooms			
Are there enough?	___	___	___
Will your furniture fit?	___	___	___
Is there adequate closet space?	___	___	___
Are noise levels low at night?	___	___	___
Is there sufficient privacy?	___	___	___
Is there adequate ventilation?	___	___	___

Living Room			
Is it attractive and spacious?	___	___	___
Is the lighting good?	___	___	___
Is there adequate privacy?	___	___	___
Does the front door open directly into the living room (and let in winter's chill)?	___	___	___
Is walk-through traffic minimized by proper room arrangement?	___	___	___

BUYING A HOME?
HERE'S WHAT TO LOOK FOR (cont'd)

Windows and Doors	Yes	No	Adequate
Do all windows and doors open and close easily, yet fit snugly?	___	___	___
Are they weather-stripped?	___	___	___
Is hardware in good condition?	___	___	___
Are screens, storm windows, and storm doors provided?	___	___	___

Dining Room	Yes	No	Adequate
Is it large enough for entertaining?	___	___	___
Is it close to the kitchen?	___	___	___
Will your furniture fit in?	___	___	___
Will furniture interfere with traffic?	___	___	___

Kitchen	Yes	No	Adequate
Are there warranties still in effect on appliances?	___	___	___
Are sink drainage and water pressure good?	___	___	___
Are there sufficient electrical outlets?	___	___	___
Are outlets conveniently placed?	___	___	___
Is there sufficient storage and counter space?	___	___	___

Floors and Walls	Yes	No	Adequate
Are all floors level, properly laid, and finished?	___	___	___
Do you feel any cracks in the floor when walking?	___	___	___
Are there any spaces between floors and baseboards?	___	___	___

BUYING A HOME?
HERE'S WHAT TO LOOK FOR (cont'd)

Basement	Yes	No	Adequate
In foundation walls, particularly around the windows, is there evidence of cracks or repairs?	___	___	___
Is all piping fully insulated?	___	___	___
Are water pipes made of durable copper or brass?	___	___	___
Are there signs of dampness?	___	___	___
Is there adequate ventilation and light?	___	___	___
If the ceiling beams are exposed, are there any signs of sag or rot?	___	___	___

Outside of House

	Yes	No	Adequate
Does it need painting?	___	___	___
Are leaders and gutters in good condition?	___	___	___
Is the roof in good condition?	___	___	___
Are there broken or missing shingles?	___	___	___
Are there signs of leaks in the attic? If possible, inspect the attic during or immediately after a rainstorm.	___	___	___
Are lawns and landscaping healthy and attractively placed?	___	___	___
Are walks and driveways in good condition?	___	___	___

General Observations

	Yes	No	Adequate
Is the layout of the rooms good?	___	___	___
Are bathrooms conveniently located?	___	___	___
Are there adequate electrical outlets?	___	___	___
Is there adequate storage space?	___	___	___
If there is a fireplace; does it work?	___	___	___
Is the water heater large enough for your family's needs?	___	___	___

TECHNICAL/FINANCIAL QUESTIONS TO CONSIDER WHEN BUYING A HOME

Exactly what property, real and personal, is included in the purchase?
___
___
___

Is the seller to furnish a marketable title?
___

What are the terms of payment?
___

Is an abstract of title to be furnished; if so, who is to pay for its extension to date?
___

Do mechanic's or materialman's liens exist against the property? Has there been any work or labor done or material furnished on the land or buildings within the last 120 days which have not been paid for, and which might be a basis for liens?
___
___

What kind of deed must the seller give?
___

Are there unpaid real estate taxes or special assessments? If so, who pays them?
___

When is the purchaser to have possession?
___

What zoning regulations affect the property?
___

TECHNICAL/FINANCIAL QUESTIONS TO CONSIDER WHEN BUYING A HOME (cont'd)

Are there any easements or restrictions on the property?

_____

_____

Have the utilities, sewer, and pavement been installed and paid for?

_____

Where are the boundaries? Are all of the improvements within the boundaries? If a survey is needed, who is to pay for it?

_____

_____

Are there any mortgages on the property? If so, what are the terms and method of payment? Are any of the mortgage payments past due?

_____

_____

Are there any other liens on the property such as judgment or income tax liens?

_____

How much insurance is in force and how is it to be prorated?

_____

_____

Who pays the salesman's commission, and for the documentary stamps needed in the transaction?

_____

A SAMPLE REAL ESTATE CONTRACT OF SALE

Articles of Agreement, made the _____ day of _____ in the year One Thousand Nine Hundred and _____ between _____, residing at _____ in the _____ of _____ in the County of _____ and State of _____ hereinafter referred to as the Seller; and _____, residing at _____ in the _____ ____ of _____ in the County of _____ and State of _____ _____ hereinafter referred to as the Purchaser;

Witnesseth, that the Seller, for and in consideration of the sum of _____, to be paid and satisfied as hereinafter mentioned, and also in consideration of the covenants and agreements hereinafter mentioned, made and entered into by the Purchaser, doth agree to and with the said Purchaser, that the Seller will well and sufficiently convey to the said Purchaser by Deed of _____ free from all encumbrance except as hereinafter mentioned, on or before the _____ day of _____ next ensuing the date hereof,

All _____ certain lot__, tract__, or parcel__ of land and premises together with the buildings thereon and the appurtenances thereto appertaining, hereinafter particularly described, situate, lying and being in the _____ of _____ in the County of _____ and State of New Jersey.

And it is further Agreed, by the parties hereto, that the said Deed _____ ____ shall be delivered and received at _____ between the hours of __ o'clock in the ____ noon and ____ o'clock in the ____ noon on the said ____ day of _____ next ensuing the date hereof.

The rents of said premises, insurance premiums, premiums or bonus for Building and Loan Mortgage, water rents, taxes, and interest on Mortgages, if any, shall be adjusted, apportioned and allowed as of the day of delivery of said deed.

Gas and electric fixtures, air conditioning or cooling system, refrigerating system, gas or oil burners, stoves, water heaters, chandeliers, carpets, linoleum, mats and matting in halls, screens, shades, awnings, ash cans, television and radio aerial equipment, heating apparatus, if any, and all other personal property appurtenant to or used in the operation of said premises is represented to be owned by Seller and is included in this sale.

The risk of loss or damage to said premises by fire or otherwise until the delivery of said deed is assumed by the Seller.

Dated:_____, 19__

Signed:

_____
Seller

_____
Buyer

PAPERS THAT MAY BE NEEDED WHEN YOU CLOSE YOUR REAL ESTATE SALE

A CHECKLIST	Yes	Not Needed
The deed	_____	_____
The most recent property tax bill and receipt (if paid)	_____	_____
Insurance policy on property	_____	_____
Termite and wood rot inspection report	_____	_____
Documents on liens (removed or existing)	_____	_____
Bill of sale for personal property	_____	_____
Survey map	_____	_____
Deed tax stamps	_____	_____
Statements on remaining debts that buyer will assume	_____	_____
IN THE CASE OF INCOME PROPERTY		
Rent schedules	_____	_____
Existing leases	_____	_____
Current expenses	_____	_____
Letters advising tenants of new ownership	_____	_____
Have you kept copies?	_____	_____

A CHECKLIST ON SOLE AND JOINT OWNERSHIP OF PROPERTY

Point of Comparison	Sole Ownership	Joint Ownership
Lifetime control	Full	Divided
Postmortem control	Yes	No
Power to will	Full	None
Income from property	All	Shared
Tax on creation	None	Possible gift tax; possible income tax
Tax on termination	Possible gift tax; possible income tax	Possible gift tax; possible income tax
Inclusion in estate	All	All, unless survivor shows contribution
Cash availability on death of owner	Delayed	Immediate or as soon as waiver of state tax lien obtained
Unintended over-qualification for marital deduction	No real danger	Danger if substantial joint property
Need for will	Yes, unless statutory disposition is OK	Same as sole ownership unless no possible other property interests
Administration expenses	Included in computing expenses and fees	Generally not included in computation
Unwinding	No special problem	Legal problems on top of tax problems
Creditors' claims	Fully subject to	Free under some state laws

THE FAMILY HOME

YOUR COMPLETE GUIDE AND RECORD

OUR HOME

Location and physical description of land, dwelling, and other improvements _____
_____
_____
_____
_____
_____
_____
_____

Legal description _____
_____
_____
_____

Date purchased _____ Date moved in _____

Purchase price _____ Down payment _____

Value of structure _____ Value of land _____

Value of fixtures, furnishings, carpets, appliances, etc.
_____
_____
_____

Closing costs _____
_____
_____
_____

OUR HOME (cont'd)

First and second mortgages or agreement of sale (include with whom—name and address—mortgage number, interest rate, and terms) _____

_____

_____

_____

_____

Refinancing _____

Previous owners _____

_____

_____

Current co-owners _____

Realty company _____

Address _____

Realty agent _____ Telephone _____

Escrow agency _____ Telephone _____

Architect _____ Telephone _____

Contractor _____ Telephone _____

Locations of deeds, licenses, tax receipts, title assessment, termite report, closing statements, blueprints, mortgage papers, and other important papers _____

_____

_____

_____

_____

_____

HOME IMPROVEMENTS

Date	Type of Improvement	Contractor	Est. Cost	Actual Cost

HOUSEHOLD INVENTORY—

Room by Room Protection in Case of Fire,
Theft, Other Loss, Sale, Bequest, Etc.

LIVING ROOM

Item	Serial Number	Cost	Date Purchased	Present Value	Date

HOUSEHOLD INVENTORY—

HOUSEHOLD INVENTORY (cont'd)

DINING ROOM

Item	Serial Number	Cost	Date Purchased	Present Value	Date

HOUSEHOLD INVENTORY (cont'd)

LIBRARY, DEN, OR STUDY

Item	Serial Number	Cost	Date Purchased	Present Value	Date

HOUSEHOLD INVENTORY (cont'd)

REC OR FAMILY ROOM

Item	Serial Number	Cost	Date Purchased	Present Value	Date

HOUSEHOLD INVENTORY (cont'd)

HALLS, SUNROOMS, PORCHES

Item	Serial Number	Cost	Date Purchased	Present Value	Date

HOUSEHOLD INVENTORY (cont'd)

BATHROOM(S)

Item	Serial Number	Cost	Date Purchased	Present Value	Date

HOUSEHOLD INVENTORY (cont'd)

BEDROOM(S)

Item	Serial Number	Cost	Date Purchased	Present Value	Date

HOUSEHOLD INVENTORY (cont'd)

SEWING ROOM

Item	Serial Number	Cost	Date Purchased	Present Value	Date

HOUSEHOLD INVENTORY (cont'd)

KITCHEN

Item	Serial Number	Cost	Date Purchased	Present Value	Date

HOUSEHOLD INVENTORY (cont'd)

BREAKFAST ROOM

Item	Serial Number	Cost	Date Purchased	Present Value	Date

HOUSEHOLD INVENTORY (cont'd)

PANTRY AND LAUNDRY ROOM

Item	Serial Number	Cost	Date Purchased	Present Value	Date

HOUSEHOLD INVENTORY (cont'd)

ATTIC

Item	Serial Number	Cost	Date Purchased	Present Value	Date

HOUSEHOLD INVENTORY (cont'd)

BASEMENT

Item	Serial Number	Cost	Date Purchased	Present Value	Date

HOUSEHOLD INVENTORY (cont'd)

GARAGE

Item	Serial Number	Cost	Date Purchased	Present Value	Date

HOUSEHOLD INVENTORY SUMMARY

	Total Orig. Cost	Date	Est. of Present Value	Date	Est. of Present Value
Living Room					
Dining Room					
Library, Den, or Study					
Rec or Family Room					
Halls, Sunrooms, Porches					
Bathroom(s)					
Bedroom(s)					
Sewing Room					
Kitchen					
Breakfast Room					
Pantry and Laundry Room					
Attic					
Basement					
Garage					
GRAND TOTALS					

DID YOU REMEMBER?

- air conditioners
- bar equipment, including wines and liquors
- clocks
- decorative items
- fireplace fixtures
- floor coverings, including pads
- interior furniture
- lawn decorations
- lawn furniture
- valuable lighting fixtures
- radios
- sewing machines and equipment
- tape and stereo equipment
- televisions
- typewriters
- vacuum cleaners
- window accessories
- workshop machines

APPLIANCES AND WARRANTIES

Appliance _____ Date purchased _____

From _____

_____ Tel. no. _____

Warranty no. _____ Cost _____

Warranty stored in _____

Price _____

Repaired (date) _____ By _____

Appliance _____ Date purchased _____

From _____

_____ Tel. no. _____

Warranty no. _____ Cost _____

Warranty stored in _____

Price _____

Repaired (date) _____ By _____

APPLIANCES AND WARRANTIES

Appliance _____ Date purchased _____

From _____

_____ Tel. no. _____

Warranty no. _____ Cost _____

Warranty stored in _____

Price _____

Repaired (date) _____ By _____

Appliance _____ Date purchased _____

From _____

_____ Tel. no. _____

Warranty no. _____ Cost _____

Warranty stored in _____

Price _____

Repaired (date) _____ By _____

APPLIANCES AND WARRANTIES

Appliance _____ Date purchased _____

From _____

_____ Tel. no. _____

Warranty no. _____ Cost _____

Warranty stored in _____

Price _____

Repaired (date) _____ By _____

Appliance _____ Date purchased _____

From _____

_____ Tel. no. _____

Warranty no. _____ Cost _____

Warranty stored in _____

Price _____

Repaired (date) _____ By _____

APPLIANCES AND WARRANTIES

Appliance _____ Date purchased _____

From _____

_____ Tel. no. _____

Warranty no. _____ Cost _____

Warranty stored in _____

Price _____

Repaired (date) _____ By _____

Appliance _____ Date purchased _____

From _____

_____ Tel. no. _____

Warranty no. _____ Cost _____

Warranty stored in _____

Price _____

Repaired (date) _____ By _____

APPLIANCES AND WARRANTIES

Appliance _____ Date purchased _____

From _____

_____ Tel. no. _____

Warranty no. _____ Cost _____

Warranty stored in _____

Price _____

Repaired (date) _____ By _____

Appliance _____ Date purchased _____

From _____

_____ Tel. no. _____

Warranty no. _____ Cost _____

Warranty stored in _____

Price _____

Repaired (date) _____ By _____

APPLIANCES AND WARRANTIES

Appliance _____ Date purchased _____

From _____

_____ Tel. no. _____

Warranty no. _____ Cost _____

Warranty stored in _____

Price _____

Repaired (date) _____ By _____

Appliance _____ Date purchased _____

From _____

_____ Tel. no. _____

Warranty no. _____ Cost _____

Warranty stored in _____

Price _____

Repaired (date) _____ By _____

OTHER PERSONAL PROPERTY

Type _____ Make _____

ID or warr. no. _____ Purchase date _____

Price _____ Sales date _____ Price _____

Type _____ Make _____

ID or warr. no. _____ Purchase date _____

Price _____ Sales date _____ Price _____

Type _____ Make _____

ID or warr. no. _____ Purchase date _____

Price _____ Sales date _____ Price _____

Type _____ Make _____

ID or warr. no. _____ Purchase date _____

Price _____ Sales date _____ Price _____

Type _____ Make _____

ID or warr. no. _____ Purchase date _____

Price _____ Sales date _____ Price _____

Type _____ Make _____

ID or warr. no. _____ Purchase date _____

Price _____ Sales date _____ Price _____

Type _____ Make _____

ID or warr. no. _____ Purchase date _____

Price _____ Sales date _____ Price _____

OTHER PERSONAL PROPERTY

Type _____ Make _____

ID or warr. no. _____ Purchase date _____

Price _____ Sales date _____ Price _____

Type _____ Make _____

ID or warr. no. _____ Purchase date _____

Price _____ Sales date _____ Price _____

Type _____ Make _____

ID or warr. no. _____ Purchase date _____

Price _____ Sales date _____ Price _____

Type _____ Make _____

ID or warr. no. _____ Purchase date _____

Price _____ Sales date _____ Price _____

Type _____ Make _____

ID or warr. no. _____ Purchase date _____

Price _____ Sales date _____ Price _____

Type _____ Make _____

ID or warr. no. _____ Purchase date _____

Price _____ Sales date _____ Price _____

Type _____ Make _____

ID or warr. no. _____ Purchase date _____

Price _____ Sales date _____ Price _____

GENERAL HOME MAINTENANCE AND REPAIRS

Don't forget:

Masonry	Plumbing	Pool service
Carpentry	Electric	Appliance service
Roofing	Heating	Housecleaning
Painting	Landscaping	Air conditioning

Date	Type of Maintenance/Repairs	Contractor	Est. Cost	Actual Cost

GENERAL HOME MAINTENANCE AND REPAIRS

Date	Type of Maintenance/ Repairs	Contractor	Est. Cost	Actual Cost

PROPERTY AND OTHER TAXES

Date Rec'd	Type of Tax or Assessment	Amount	Date Paid

PROPERTY AND OTHER TAXES

Date Rec'd	Type of Tax or Assessment	Amount	Date Paid

HOME OFFICE EXPENSES: INFORMATION FOR CALCULATING DEDUCTIBILITY

You work at home. You use one room exclusively for the conduct of your business. Your accountant will be able to tell you how much you can deduct. Those calculations are done with reference to the tax laws in effect in the particular year. But your accountant will need some details. The answers to the following questions should provide the required information.

Step 1 - Percentage the home is used in business

   1) Rooms used for business   _____

   2) Total number of rooms in home   _____

   3) Divide (1) by (2) (percentage of business use of home)   _____

Step 2 - Time business portion used to provide services (e.g., for day-care facilities)

   1) Total hours used for facility
      (____days × ____hrs.)   _____

   2) Total hours available
      (24 hrs. × 365 days)   8760

   3) Divide (1) by (2) (percentage time used)   _____

Step 3 - Computing depreciation on your home

   1) Adjusted basis of home (less salvage)   _____

   2) Estimated useful life   _____

   3) Divide (1) by (2) (depreciation for home)   _____

Step 4 - Allocating expenses for business use

   1) Direct expenses

      a) Repairs to business portion of home   _____

      b) Painting of business portion of home   _____

      c) Other direct expenses   _____

      d) Total   _____

   2) Indirect business expenses (multiply total expense by percentage in Step 1; for day-care facilities, multiply by percentage in Step 1, then by percentage in Step 2)

Expense	Total Expense	Business Portion
Real estate taxes[1]	_____	_____
Mortgage interest[1]	_____	_____
Lights	_____	_____

HOME OFFICE EXPENSES: INFORMATION FOR CALCULATING DEDUCTIBILITY (cont'd)

Expense	Total Expense	Business Portion
Heating	_____	_____
Insurance, 1 yr.	_____	_____
Exterior painting	_____	_____
Roof repair	_____	_____
Depreciation on home (Step 3)	_____	_____
Miscellaneous	_____	_____
Total business deduction related to your home (add totals in (1) & (2))		_____

Step 5 - Deduction limitation

1) Gross income from business[2]   _____

2) Less business portion (total expense multiplied by percentage in Step 1 or in the case of day-care facilities, total expense multiplied in Step 1, then by percentage in Step 2 of the following items:

    a) Real estate taxes   _____

    b) Mortgage interest   _____

    c) Casualty loss(es)   _____   _____

3) Total deduction limitation   _____

Step 6 - Compare total business expenses in Step 4 to total limitation in Step 5. If the expenses exceed the total limitation, the excess is not deductible; however, if the total limitation exceeds the total business expenses, all expenses related to business use of your home are deductible.

---

[1]Remaining portion of real estate taxes and mortgage interest after the percentage business deduction is the personal portion deduction on Schedule A, Form 1040.

[2]When gross income is derived both from the use of your home and from the use of other facilities, a reasonable allocation will have to be made to determine what portion of the gross income is allocable to your home.

YOUR HOME SECURITY CHECKLIST

Crime prevention experts say you can help safeguard the family homestead in various ways. One good way is to inspect your premises periodically. Your security checks will focus on places that might slow down, stop, or deter a potential burglar—or that might, conversely, provide cover or give entry and make the burglar's job easier. On the following checklist, an "S" for Satisfactory means you feel the item functions or is arranged so as to contribute to your security. A "U" for Unsatisfactory means the opposite. You should, if possible, take corrective action on the U's.

Doors

- Main entrance   S U
- Side door   S U
- Back door   S U
- Basement door   S U
- Other door (_____)   S U
- Other door (_____)   S U
- Sliding door (inside)   S U
- Sliding door (outside)   S U

Windows

- Double hung   S U
- Sliding   S U
- Casement   S U
- Louver   S U
- Other (_____)   S U
- Lighting   S U
- Alarm system   Yes No
- Misc. opening (_____)   S U
- Misc. opening (_____)   S U
- Misc. opening (_____)   S U

Outside Area

- Front yard   S U
- Side yard   S U
- Back yard   S U
- Fence   S U
- Shrubs   S U
- Gates   S U
- Lighting   S U
- Laundry area   S U
- Trash disposal area   S U

Hallways   S U

Parking Areas   S U

Garage   S U
- Door   S U
- Windows   S U
- Lighting   S U

MOVING? CHECK YOUR PREPARATIONS CAREFULLY

A CHECKLIST

_____ Notify post office of move and fill out change of address cards; send change to friends, businesses.

_____ Get all medical and dental records.

_____ Check and clear tax assessments.

_____ Have your W-2's and other tax forms forwarded.

_____ Transfer insurance records; check auto licensing requirements.

_____ Notify school and make arrangements for sending transcripts of school records to new school.

_____ Have letters of introduction written.

_____ Arrange for transfer of jewelry and important documents.

_____ Arrange shipment of pets and any immunization records.

_____ Make travel plans.

_____ Get hotel reservations and make note to reconfirm.

14 DAYS BEFORE YOUR MOVE

_____ Collect all items to be cleaned or repaired.

_____ Return things borrowed, collect things lent.

_____ Transfer bank accounts and release safe deposit box.

_____ Arrange to disconnect utility services.

_____ Arrange to connect utility service at new home.

_____ Make arrangements to have heavy appliances serviced for move.

_____ Give away articles you don't plan to take along. Give to charitable organizations; get signed receipt for tax purposes.

7 DAYS BEFORE YOUR MOVE

_____ Dispose of all flammables.

_____ Have car inspected and serviced.

_____ Select traveling games.

_____ Set things aside to pack in car.

_____ Take down curtains, rods, shelves, TV antenna if agreement with owner authorizes this.

_____ Start packing; include suitcases you can live out of, if necessary, for the first day in your new home.

_____ Line up a baby sitter for moving day so you can look after moving.

MOVING? CHECK YOUR PREPARATIONS CAREFULLY (cont'd)

____ In a special carton place items you will need in the first few hours in your new home: soap, towels, coffee, cooking pot, etc. Mark this carton with sticker "Load Last - Unload First!"

____ Make up special cartons with "Do not move" for articles to be taken in car.

DAY BEFORE MOVING

____ Empty and defrost your refrigerator and freezer. Let them air at least 24 hours. Also, clean and air your range.

____ Line up a simple breakfast for next morning that won't require refrigeration or much cooking. Use paper plates.

____ Finish packing personal belongings, but leave out the alarm clock!

____ Get a good night's rest.

MOVING DAY

____ Be on hand the day of your move, or have someone there authorized to answer questions.

____ Strip your beds, but leave fitted bottom sheets on your mattresses.

____ Accompany the van operator while he inventories your possessions to be moved.

____ Make last-minute check on your appliance to see that they have been serviced.

____ Sign (and save your copy of) bills of lading and make sure delivery address and place to locate you enroute are correct.

____ Ask that you be advised of final cost. If you have not arranged for time payment for move, or your company is not paying for it, make sure you'll have the needed cash, money order, or certified check to pay before van is unloaded at destination. Carriers require payment before unloading.

____ Before leaving house, check each room and closet; make sure windows are down and lights out.

MOVING-IN TIPS

____ Upon arrival at new location, call the moving agent immediately to leave address and phone number where you can be reached at specified times.

____ Be on hand at unloading and have a plan for placement of your furniture.

____ Check all electrical fuses. Sometimes pennies have been used as substitutes!

____ Check the condition of your belongings. If any items are missing or damaged, note this on your inventory sheet and shipping papers; report such information to your moving agent who will take care of it for you.

____ If your utilities haven't been connected, call for this service, and have your appliances checked for proper operation.

VACATION OR SECOND HOME RECORDS

First and second mortgages or agreement of sale (include with whom—name and address—mortgage number, interest rate, and terms) _____

_____

_____

Refinancing _____

Previous owners _____

_____

Current co-owners _____

Realty company _____

Address _____

Realty agent _____ Telephone _____

Escrow agency _____ Telephone _____

Architect _____ Telephone _____

Contractor _____ Telephone _____

Location of deeds, licenses, tax receipts, title assessment, termite report, closing statements, blueprints, mortgage papers, and other important papers _____

_____

_____

_____

_____

_____

VACATION OR
SECOND HOME RECORDS (cont'd)

Location and physical description of land and dwelling _____

_____

_____

_____

_____

_____

_____

Legal description_____

_____

_____

_____

Date purchased _____ Date moved in _____

Purchase price _____ Down payment _____

Value of structure _____ Value of land _____

Values of fixtures, furnishings, carpets, etc. _____

_____

_____

_____

Closing costs _____

_____

_____

REAL ESTATE REPAIRS—VACATION/SECOND HOME

Don't forget:

Air conditioning	Plumbing	Masonry
Pool service	Electric	Carpentry
Appliance service	Heating	Roofing
Housecleaning	Landscaping	Painting

Date	Type of Maintenance/Repairs	Contractor	Est. Cost	Actual Cost

REAL ESTATE REPAIRS—
VACATION/SECOND HOME (cont'd)

Date	Type of Maintenance/Repairs	Contractor	Est. Cost	Actual Cost

PART III

YOUR FAMILY HISTORY, BABY BOOK, INSURANCE, AND OTHER IMPORTANT MATTERS

YOUR FAMILY HISTORY, BABY BOOK, INSURANCE, AND OTHER IMPORTANT MATTERS

Kids see their siblings in different lights. Where Johnny believes his sister makes a perfect punching bag, little Rosie views her tiny brother as a living, moving doll. Needing parental and family love, many children take confidence and a sense of security from their home relationships. A typical comment from a fourth-grader's theme:

"Kids who have no familys should get mad."

Such statements give a child's-eye view of the family and its merits. The youngsters can't be blamed if the statements don't go far enough. Who understands at the age of 6 or 8 or 10 that "family" can mean marriage, divorce, childrearing, insurance, pensions, retirement, wills, estates, trusts, confirmations and bar mitzvahs, and many other things?

Who understands that "family" today may be translated in terms of family health? That may mean medical histories, perhaps from the prenatal months onward; dental, optical, and immunization records; and emergency data and instructions, especially where a family member has a special condition; and many other things.

The section on the family also includes records on births and marriages, family advisors, family identification numbers such as Social Security numbers, and a household register showing who has access to your home. Instructions to the babysitter may be all-important to parents of young children.

The family records may rank among your most important. They may become a family history. They may serve as reminders of doctor or dentist visits; they will certainly come in handy when you are filling out applications. You may use these records when your son or daughter is entering school—at any level—or going away to camp. You may need them when talking with your doctor or moving to another city.

Having sisters, and a family, involves much more than having someone to hit.

THE VIEW FROM THE FAMILY TREE

OUR FAMILY TREE

1 You
b
w
m
w

Spouse
b
w

2 Father
b
w
d
w
m
w

3 Mother
b
w
d
w

4 G-F
b
w
d
w
m
w

5 G-M
b
w
d
w

6 G-F
b
w
d
w
m
w

7 G-M
b
w
d
w

8 GGF
b
d
m

9 GGM
b
d

10 GGF
b
d
m

11 GGM
b
d

12 GGF
b
d
m

13 GGM
b
d

14 GGF
b
d
m

15 GGM
b
d

b. (born)
w. (where)
d. (died)
m. (married)

FAMILY DATA SHEET

Husband		Wife	
Born	at	Born	at
Died	at	Died	at
Married	at		
Buried		Buried	
Religion		Religion	
Father		Father	
Born	at	Born	at
Died	at	Died	at
Married	at	Married	at
Buried		Buried	
Religion		Religion	
Mother		Mother	
Born	at	Born	at
Died	at	Died	at
Buried		Buried	
Religion		Religion	
Grandfather		Grandfather	
Born	Died	Born	Died
Grandmother		Grandmother	
Born	Died	Born	Died
Grandfather		Grandfather	
Born	Died	Born	Died
Grandmother		Grandmother	
Born	Died	Born	Died
Great Grandfather		Great Grandfather	
Born	Died	Born	Died
Great Grandmother		Great Grandmother	
Born	Died	Born	Died
Great Grandfather		Great Grandfather	
Born	Died	Born	Died
Great Grandmother		Great Grandmother	
Born	Died	Born	Died
Great Grandfather		Great Grandfather	
Born	Died	Born	Died
Great Grandmother		Great Grandmother	
Born	Died	Born	Died
Great Grandfather		Great Grandfather	
Born	Died	Born	Died
Great Grandmother		Great Grandmother	
Born	Died	Born	Died

ORAL HISTORY: TAPING GOLDEN AGERS' MEMORIES

Ever consider exploring your family's past as reflected in the recollections of a parent, grandparent, or other elderly relative? You can do it by taking what is called *oral history:* recording, usually with a tape recorder, the remembered details of experiences, events, conversations, and other family lore. Oral history could give you the perfect complement to the information you're preserving in this book.

Like most other things, oral history calls for both planning and technique. Your subject should know in advance that you will be taping thoughts and memories informally, that you will be asking questions, that you want to enrich the family's knowledge of its own past. Regarding technique, you will want to remember the five W's and one H: Who? What? When? Where? Why? How? Here is a checklist that will make your oral history more enjoyable, valuable, and useful as a record:

____ *Ask the right questions in the right way.* (Ask questions that require more of an answer than Yes or No. Ask one question at a time. Keep questions short.)

____ *Use cues and be specific.* (Ask about specific events and experiences. Try to obtain the subject's ideas and thoughts by referring to things or people he or she would have known or known about.)

____ *Use props if any are available.* (Refer to family pictures, scrapbooks, newspaper clippings, albums, heirlooms, maps, and so on. Make sure you identify such items on the tape.)

____ *Elicit emotions where possible.* (To paint in the color and sense of a bygone period or event, you should ask the subject to recall feelings and emotions.)

ORAL HISTORY:
TAPING GOLDEN AGERS' MEMORIES (cont'd)

_____ *Personal history in dialogue.* (To the extent possible, try to obtain conversations or comments, or the gists of conversations. In so doing the subject may be able to reconstruct vivid scenes.)

_____ *To fill in details, try to get physical descriptions of people, houses, other buildings, places,* almost anything. (When beginning a new subject, ask for reconstruction or elaboration of the setting. Find out what people looked like, how they dressed, and if possible go from there to personality characteristics.)

_____ *Be patient, non-argumentative, persistent, polite.* (Try to follow conversations that go off on tangents, then come back to your subject when the opportunity offers. Don't interrupt or contradict. Don't worry about a blank space on the tape if your subject wants to think something over. So as not to distract your interviewee, keep your tape recorder on throughout the interview.)

_____ *Be flexible and thoughtful.* (If you have your questions sketched out, don't hesitate to depart from them to follow up on a new theme. Limit your interview to an hour or, at the most, two hours.)

_____ *If you plan to interview more than one person, try to talk to each alone.* (A three-way conversation, or a four-way, can be confusing; or it can get off the track and out of hand.)

_____ *Carefully identify each tape by name and relationship of interviewee, the subjects covered, date, place, and time.*

FAMILY BIRTH INFORMATION

HUSBAND

Name _____

Place
of birth _____
_____

Location of
birth cert. _____
_____

WIFE

Name _____

Place
of birth _____
_____

Location of
birth cert. _____
_____

CHILDREN

Name _____

Birthdate _____

Place of
birth _____

Location of
birth cert. _____

Ht. at birth _____

Wt. at birth _____

Name _____

Birthdate _____

Place of
birth _____

Location of
birth cert. _____

Ht. at birth _____

Wt. at birth _____

Name _____

Birthdate _____

Place of
birth _____

Location of
birth cert. _____

Ht. at birth _____

Wt. at birth _____

Name _____

Birthdate _____

Place of
birth _____

Location of
birth cert. _____

Ht. at birth _____

Wt. at birth _____

FAMILY MARRIAGE INFORMATION

We were married at _____

Date _____ Married by _____

Wife's maiden name _____

Premarital agreement is located at _____

HUSBAND	**WIFE**
State of jurisdiction _____	State of jurisdiction _____
Papers located at _____	Papers located at _____
Attorney _____	Attorney _____
Telephone _____	Telephone _____
Address _____	Address _____

CHILDREN from PREVIOUS MARRIAGES:
(enter "H" or "W" into box preceding detail line)

☐ Name _____   ☐ Name _____

Birthdate _____   Birthdate _____

☐ Name _____   ☐ Name _____

Birthdate _____   Birthdate _____

☐ Name _____   ☐ Name _____

Birthdate _____   Birthdate _____

RESPONSIBILITY of ESTATE to CHILDREN of PREVIOUS MARRIAGE(S):

_____

_____

CHILDREN'S MARRIAGES

Child's name _____   Child's name _____

Spouse _____   Spouse _____

Bride's maiden
name _____   Bride's maiden
name _____

Marriage date _____   Marriage date _____

Place of marriage _____   Place of marriage _____

Married by _____   Married by _____

Child's name _____   Child's name _____

Spouse _____   Spouse _____

Bride's maiden
name _____   Bride's maiden
name _____

Marriage date _____   Marriage date _____

Place of marriage _____   Place of marriage _____

Married by _____   Married by _____

Other information related to children's marriages (in-laws, etc.) _____

_____

_____

ADOPTION RECORDS

Name _____

Natural parents _____

_____

Adoptive parents _____

_____

Placement date _____ Adoption date _____

Name and address of court _____

_____

Name of judge _____

Location of adoption records _____

_____

Agency _____

Address _____

_____

Remarks _____

_____

_____

_____

ADOPTION RECORDS

Name _____

Natural parents _____
_____

Adoptive parents _____
_____

Placement date _____ Adoption date _____

Name and address of court _____
_____

Name of judge _____

Location of adoption records _____
_____

Agency _____

Address _____
_____

Remarks _____
_____
_____
_____

CITIZENSHIP

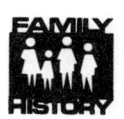

FAMILY HISTORY

Registration no. ______________________________

Native country ______________________________

Date and port of entry ______________________________

Date of naturalization ______________________________

Place of naturalization ______________________________

Location of naturalization records ______________________________

____

____

Naturalization certificate no. ______________________________

If derived, parents' certificate no(s). ______________________________

____

____

Registration no. ______________________________

Native country ______________________________

Date and port of entry ______________________________

Date of naturalization ______________________________

Place of naturalization ______________________________

Location of naturalization records ______________________________

____

____

Naturalization certificate no. ______________________________

If derived, parents' certificate no(s). ______________________________

____

____

CITIZENSHIP

Registration no. _____

Native country _____

Date and port of entry _____

Date of naturalization _____

Place of naturalization _____

Location of naturalization records _____

_____

_____

Naturalization certificate no. _____

If derived, parents' certificate no(s). _____

_____

_____

Registration no. _____

Native country _____

Date and port of entry _____

Date of naturalization _____

Place of naturalization _____

Location of naturalization records _____

_____

_____

Naturalization certificate no. _____

If derived, parents' certificate no(s). _____

_____

_____

IDENTIFICATION

FAMILY HISTORY

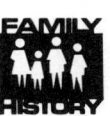

Fingerprints, palmprints, footprints, etc.,
at birth or later in life

Date ____________________ Type of ident. ____________________

Person making identification ____________________

Location of prints ____________________

____

Date ____________________ Type of ident. ____________________

Person making identification ____________________

Location of prints ____________________

____

Date ____________________ Type of ident. ____________________

Person making identification ____________________

Location of prints ____________________

____

Date ____________________ Type of ident. ____________________

Person making identification ____________________

Location of prints ____________________

____

Date ____________________ Type of ident. ____________________

Person making identification ____________________

Location of prints ____________________

____

RELIGIOUS AFFILIATIONS

Family member _____

Religion _____

Religious name _____ Named for _____

Godmother _____

Godfather _____

Baptism: Date _____ Where certificate kept _____
_____

Clergyman officiating _____

Church _____

First communion: Date _____ Where certificate kept _____
_____

Clergyman officiating _____

Church _____

Confirmation: Date _____ Where certificate kept _____
_____

Clergyman officiating _____

Church _____

RELIGIOUS AFFILIATIONS (cont'd)

Bar (Bat) Mitzvah: Date _____ Synagogue _____

Rabbi officiating _____

Cantor officiating _____

Remarks _____

OTHER CEREMONIES

_____
_____
_____
_____
_____

RELIGIOUS EDUCATION AND ACTIVITIES

_____
_____
_____
_____
_____
_____

RELIGIOUS AFFILIATIONS

Family member _____

Religion _____

Religious name _____ Named for _____

Godmother _____

Godfather _____

Baptism: Date _____ Where certificate kept _____

_____

Clergyman officiating _____

Church _____

First communion: Date _____ Where certificate kept _____

_____

Clergyman officiating _____

Church _____

Confirmation: Date _____ Where certificate kept _____

_____

Clergyman officiating _____

Church _____

RELIGIOUS AFFILIATIONS (cont'd)

Bar (Bat) Mitzvah: Date _____ Synagogue _____

Rabbi officiating _____

Cantor officiating _____

Remarks _____

OTHER CEREMONIES

_____

_____

_____

_____

RELIGIOUS EDUCATION AND ACTIVITIES

_____

_____

_____

_____

_____

RELIGIOUS AFFILIATIONS

Family member _____

Religion _____

Religious name _____ Named for _____

Godmother _____

Godfather _____

Baptism: Date _____ Where certificate kept _____

_____

Clergyman officiating _____

Church _____

First communion: Date _____ Where certificate kept _____

_____

Clergyman officiating _____

Church _____

Confirmation: Date _____ Where certificate kept _____

_____

Clergyman officiating _____

Church _____

RELIGIOUS AFFILIATIONS (cont'd)

Bar (Bat)
Mitzvah: Date _____ Synagogue _____

Rabbi officiating _____

Cantor officiating _____

Remarks _____

OTHER CEREMONIES

_____

_____

_____

_____

_____

RELIGIOUS EDUCATION AND ACTIVITIES

_____

_____

_____

_____

_____

RELIGIOUS AFFILIATIONS

Family member _____

Religion _____

Religious name _____ Named for _____

Godmother _____

Godfather _____

Baptism: Date _____ Where certificate kept _____

_____

Clergyman officiating _____

Church _____

First communion: Date _____ Where certificate kept _____

_____

Clergyman officiating _____

Church _____

Confirmation: Date _____ Where certificate kept _____

_____

Clergyman officiating _____

Church _____

RELIGIOUS AFFILIATIONS (cont'd)

Bar (Bat) Mitzvah: Date _____ Synagogue _____

Rabbi officiating _____

Cantor officiating _____

Remarks _____

OTHER CEREMONIES

_____
_____
_____
_____
_____

RELIGIOUS EDUCATION AND ACTIVITIES

_____
_____
_____
_____
_____
_____

RELIGIOUS AFFILIATIONS

Family member _____

Religion _____

Religious name _____ Named for _____

Godmother _____

Godfather _____

Baptism: Date _____ Where certificate kept _____

_____

Clergyman officiating _____

Church _____

First communion: Date _____ Where certificate kept _____

_____

Clergyman officiating _____

Church _____

Confirmation: Date _____ Where certificate kept _____

_____

Clergyman officiating _____

Church _____

RELIGIOUS AFFILIATIONS (cont'd)

Bar (Bat) Mitzvah: Date _____ Synagogue _____

Rabbi officiating _____

Cantor officiating _____

Remarks _____

OTHER CEREMONIES

_____
_____
_____
_____
_____
_____

RELIGIOUS EDUCATION AND ACTIVITIES

_____
_____
_____
_____
_____
_____

RELIGIOUS AFFILIATIONS

Family member _____

Religion _____

Religious name _____ Named for _____

Godmother _____

Godfather _____

Baptism: Date _____ Where certificate kept _____

_____

Clergyman officiating _____

Church _____

First communion: Date _____ Where certificate kept _____

_____

Clergyman officiating _____

Church _____

Confirmation: Date _____ Where certificate kept _____

_____

Clergyman officiating _____

Church _____

RELIGIOUS AFFILIATIONS (cont'd)

Bar (Bat)
Mitzvah: Date _____ Synagogue _____

Rabbi officiating _____

Cantor officiating _____

Remarks _____

OTHER CEREMONIES

_____

_____

_____

_____

_____

RELIGIOUS EDUCATION AND ACTIVITIES

_____

_____

_____

_____

_____

ACTIVITIES—COMMUNITY, SOCIAL, RELIGIOUS, OTHER

Family member _____ Activity _____

Name of organization _____

Address _____ Telephone _____

Your participation (include offices held) _____

_____

Events, leaders, credentials, and other information _____

_____

Family member _____ Activity _____

Name of organization _____

Address _____ Telephone _____

Your participation (include offices held) _____

_____

Events, leaders, credentials, and other information _____

_____

Family member _____ Activity _____

Name of organization _____

Address _____ Telephone _____

Your participation (include offices held) _____

_____

Events, leaders, credentials, and other information _____

_____

ACTIVITIES—COMMUNITY, SOCIAL, RELIGIOUS, OTHER

Family member _____ Activity _____

Name of organization _____

Address _____ Telephone _____

Your participation (include offices held) _____
_____

Events, leaders, credentials, and other information _____
_____

Family member _____ Activity _____

Name of organization _____

Address _____ Telephone _____

Your participation (include offices held) _____
_____

Events, leaders, credentials, and other information _____
_____

Family member _____ Activity _____

Name of organization _____

Address _____ Telephone _____

Your participation (include offices held) _____
_____

Events, leaders, credentials, and other information _____
_____

ACTIVITIES—COMMUNITY, SOCIAL, RELIGIOUS, OTHER

Family member _____ Activity _____

Name of organization _____

Address _____ Telephone _____

Your participation (include offices held) _____
_____

Events, leaders, credentials, and other information _____
_____

Family member _____ Activity _____

Name of organization _____

Address _____ Telephone _____

Your participation (include offices held) _____
_____

Events, leaders, credentials, and other information _____
_____

Family member _____ Activity _____

Name of organization _____

Address _____ Telephone _____

Your participation (include offices held) _____
_____

Events, leaders, credentials, and other information _____
_____

ACTIVITIES—COMMUNITY, SOCIAL, RELIGIOUS, OTHER

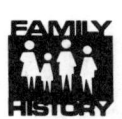

FAMILY HISTORY

Family member ______________________ Activity ______________________

Name of organization ____

Address ______________________________ Telephone ________________

Your participation (include offices held) ____________________________

____

Events, leaders, credentials, and other information __________________

____

Family member ______________________ Activity ______________________

Name of organization ____

Address ______________________________ Telephone ________________

Your participation (include offices held) ____________________________

____

Events, leaders, credentials,and other information __________________

____

Family member ______________________ Activity ______________________

Name of organization ____

Address ______________________________ Telephone ________________

Your participation (include offices held) ____________________________

____

Events, leaders, credentials, and other information __________________

____

ACTIVITIES—COMMUNITY, SOCIAL, RELIGIOUS, OTHER

Family member _____ Activity _____

Name of organization _____

Address _____ Telephone _____

Your participation (include offices held) _____
_____

Events, leaders, credentials, and other information _____
_____

Family member _____ Activity _____

Name of organization _____

Address _____ Telephone _____

Your participation (include offices held) _____
_____

Events, leaders, credentials,and other information _____
_____

Family member _____ Activity _____

Name of organization _____

Address _____ Telephone _____

Your participation (include offices held) _____
_____

Events, leaders, credentials, and other information _____
_____

ACTIVITIES—COMMUNITY, SOCIAL, RELIGIOUS, OTHER

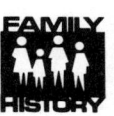

FAMILY HISTORY

Family member ______________________ Activity ______________________

Name of organization ____

Address ______________________________ Telephone ________________

Your participation (include offices held) ____________________________

____

Events, leaders, credentials, and other information ___________________

____

Family member ______________________ Activity ______________________

Name of organization ____

Address ______________________________ Telephone ________________

Your participation (include offices held) ____________________________

____

Events, leaders, credentials,and other information ____________________

____

Family member ______________________ Activity ______________________

Name of organization ____

Address ______________________________ Telephone ________________

Your participation (include offices held) ____________________________

____

Events, leaders, credentials, and other information ___________________

____

FAVORITE FAMILY RECIPES

A Short Guide to Great Eating

Eating habits run in families. Partly for that reason, most families have at least a few recipes that have been handed down from one generation to another. You may want to record your favorite family recipes on this and the following pages.

1. _____

2. _____

FAVORITE FAMILY RECIPES (cont'd)

3. _____

4. _____

FAVORITE FAMILY RECIPES (cont'd)

5. _____

6. _____

FAVORITE FAMILY RECIPES (cont'd)

7. _____

8. _____

FAVORITE RECIPES (cont'd)

9.

10.

FAVORITE RECIPES (cont'd)

11.

12.

YOUR BABY BOOK

OUR BABY IS BORN

We prepared for our baby by attending Expectant Parent Classes:

____yes ____no

Labor began on _____ at ____ o'clock.

I went to the hospital at ____ o'clock. Name and location of hospital_____
_____

Husband (or a significant other) was with me during labor:

____yes ____no   Labor lasted ____ hours, delivery ____ hours.

Our baby was born (date) _____ at ____ o'clock.

City _____ County _____ State _____

Attending doctors and nurses _____
_____

I was able to breastfeed and hold my baby during the first hours of life:

____yes ____no

The father was able to hold the baby during the first hours of life:

____yes ____no

Family-centered care was available at my hospital:

____yes ____no

Baby "roomed in":   ____yes ____no

Father took care of baby: ____yes ____no

Siblings visited: ____yes ____no

Additional comments _____
_____
_____
_____

WE PROUDLY PRESENT

Name _____

Named for _____

Religious ceremony _____
_____

Clergyman officiating _____

Godmother _____

Godfather _____

Those present _____
_____
_____

Attach baby's first photograph and birth announcement

IDENTIFICATION MARKS

Attach hospital identification here

| Birthmarks Location: Make drawings to show shape and size | Palmprints or Footprints |

Color of eyes at birth _____ six mos. _____ nine mos. _____

Color of hair at birth _____ six mos. _____ nine mos. _____

    brows _____

    lashes _____

Complexion _____ Shape of head _____

Birth Certificate

Place a copy of baby's birth certificate on this page. Your local or State Health Department will furnish one on your request. The birth certificate remains valuable throughout life. It provides proof of parents' and child's identities and citizenship; it establishes rights to attend school, hold public office, obtain social security number, get passports, inherit property, etc.; it also assures mother's right to a pension.

BABY'S FIRST YEAR... MENTAL, PHYSICAL, AND SOCIAL DEVELOPMENT

All children go through similar stages of development, but in their own ways and at their own rates. The age classifications given below are approximate. Wide variations occur within normal limits. Fill in the ages at which your child reaches the following typical stages, but do not try to hurry the process. Praise all efforts and accomplishments.

Newborn

_____ All limb movements are reflex responses

One month old

_____ Preferred position (usually lying on back) finds child with head turned toward favored side, with hand extended

Two months old

_____ Responds to voice with symmetrical limb movements and to noises with crying

Three months old

_____ Lifts head up 45 degrees while lying on stomach

Four months old

_____ Eyes now follow moving object

Five months old

_____ Smiles spontaneously at your face

Six months old

_____ Vocal play ("babbling") includes combinations of sounds and some repetition. Shows sensitivity to stern sounds in environment

Seven months old

_____ Maintains sitting position for long periods of time

Eight months old

_____ Withdrawal or crying when a stranger approaches. Indicates the child's ability to distinguish between the familiar and unfamiliar

Nine months old

_____ Begins to crawl (allow plenty of opportunity and space)

Ten months old

_____ Pulls self to standing position. Advanced stages of grasping and manipulating objects

Eleven months old

_____ Uses spoon, if filled for him

Twelve months old

_____ Imitates speech and musical sounds; may be saying first true words

SECOND YEAR GROWTH...
AND DEVELOPMENT

Here's how our child goes to sleep:

    We make sleep attractive by use of   ____musical toy   ____stories

    Nap times: morning from ____ to ____;   afternoon from ____ to ____

    Night sleep approximately from ____ to ____, average of ____ hours daily

    Takes favorite toy or blanket _____

Health habits:

    Brushes teeth   ____with help   ____by self   How many teeth? ____

    Handwashing after elimination at age ____

    Handwashing before meals at age ____

    Daily bath _____

Dressing—starts to help by _____

Physical activity:

    Develops body control (insert age):

        running____   jumping____   exploring____   pedals kiddie car____

        climbing____   sliding____   swinging____   kicks and throws a ball____

Here's what he has to say ... and what he means

_____

_____

_____

_____

THIRD YEAR GROWTH...
AND DEVELOPMENT

Favorite foods:

Morning	Noon	Evening	Snacks
_____	_____	_____	_____

Health habits:

Brushes teeth ____with help ____by self ____before breakfast

____after meals ____at bedtime

Elimination (if accidental, do not show disgust)

regular times at ____ and at ____; stays dry during the day at _____

Learning to: **At age of**

Speak in sentences—as tools of thought—says: _____

_____ ____

Give identification (name, address, etc.) ____

Follow simple directions ____

Dressing self:

____selects clothes to wear next day

____helps to dress self ____can undress alone

Increasing motor ability (use of muscles not well controlled): **At age of**

Walks up steps—jumps down ____

Opens door ____

Climbs ladder to slide ____

Pedals a tricycle ____

Develops new speech sounds ____

114

OUR BABY IS BORN

We prepared for our baby by attending Expectant Parent Classes:

____yes ____no

Labor began on _____ at ____ o'clock.

I went to the hospital at ____ o'clock. Name and location of hospital_____
_____

Husband (or a significant other) was with me during labor:

____yes ____no   Labor lasted ____ hours, delivery ____ hours.

Our baby was born (date) _____ at ____ o'clock.

City _____ County _____ State _____

Attending doctors and nurses _____
_____

I was able to breastfeed and hold my baby during the first hours of life:

____yes ____no

The father was able to hold the baby during the first hours of life:

____yes ____no

Family-centered care was available at my hospital:

____yes ____no

Baby "roomed in":   ____yes ____no

Father took care of baby: ____yes ____no

Siblings visited: ____yes ____no

Additional comments _____
_____
_____
_____
_____

WE PROUDLY PRESENT

Name _____

Named for _____

Religious ceremony _____
_____

Clergyman officiating _____

Godmother _____

Godfather _____

Those present _____
_____
_____

Attach baby's first photograph and birth announcement

IDENTIFICATION MARKS

Attach hospital identification here

| Birthmarks
Location: Make drawings to show shape and size | Palmprints or Footprints |

Color of eyes at birth _____ six mos. _____ nine mos. _____
Color of hair at birth _____ six mos. _____ nine mos. _____
    brows _____
    lashes _____
Complexion _____ Shape of head _____

Birth Certificate

Place a copy of baby's birth certificate on this page. Your local or State Health Department will furnish one on your request. The birth certificate remains valuable throughout life. It provides proof of parents' and child's identities and citizenship; it establishes rights to attend school, hold public office, obtain social security number, get passports, inherit property, etc.; it also assures mother's right to a pension.

BABY'S FIRST YEAR... MENTAL, PHYSICAL, AND SOCIAL DEVELOPMENT

All children go through similar stages of development, but in their own ways and at their own rates. The age classifications given below are approximate. Wide variations occur within normal limits. Fill in the ages at which your child reaches the following typical stages, but do not try to hurry the process. Praise all efforts and accomplishments.

Newborn

_____ All limb movements are reflex responses

One month old

_____ Preferred position (usually lying on back) finds child with head turned toward favored side, with hand extended

Two months old

_____ Responds to voice with symmetrical limb movements and to noises with crying

Three months old

_____ Lifts head up 45 degrees while lying on stomach

Four months old

_____ Eyes now follow moving object

Five months old

_____ Smiles spontaneously at your face

Six months old

_____ Vocal play ("babbling") includes combinations of sounds and some repetition. Shows sensitivity to stern sounds in environment

Seven months old

_____ Maintains sitting position for long periods of time

Eight months old

_____ Withdrawal or crying when a stranger approaches. Indicates the child's ability to distinguish between the familiar and unfamiliar

Nine months old

_____ Begins to crawl (allow plenty of opportunity and space)

Ten months old

_____ Pulls self to standing position. Advanced stages of grasping and manipulating objects

Eleven months old

_____ Uses spoon, if filled for him

Twelve months old

_____ Imitates speech and musical sounds; may be saying first true words

SECOND YEAR GROWTH...
AND DEVELOPMENT

Here's how our child goes to sleep:

    We make sleep attractive by use of   ____musical toy   ____stories

    Nap times: morning from ____ to ____; afternoon from ____ to ____

    Night sleep approximately from ____ to ____, average of ____ hours daily

    Takes favorite toy or blanket _____

Health habits:

    Brushes teeth   ____with help   ____by self   How many teeth? ____

    Handwashing after elimination at age ____

    Handwashing before meals at age ____

    Daily bath _____

Dressing—starts to help by _____

Physical activity:

    Develops body control (insert age):

        running____   jumping____   exploring____   pedals kiddie car____

        climbing____   sliding____   swinging____   kicks and throws a ball____

Here's what he has to say . . . and what he means

_____

_____

_____

_____

THIRD YEAR GROWTH...
AND DEVELOPMENT

Favorite foods:

Morning	Noon	Evening	Snacks
_____	_____	_____	_____

Health habits:

Brushes teeth ____with help ____by self ____before breakfast

____after meals ____at bedtime

Elimination (if accidental, do not show disgust)

regular times at ____ and at ____; stays dry during the day at _____

Learning to: **At age of**

Speak in sentences—as tools of thought—says: _____

_____ ____

Give identification (name, address, etc.) ____

Follow simple directions ____

Dressing self:

____selects clothes to wear next day

____helps to dress self ____can undress alone

Increasing motor ability (use of muscles not well controlled): **At age of**

Walks up steps—jumps down ____

Opens door ____

Climbs ladder to slide ____

Pedals a tricycle ____

Develops new speech sounds ____

OUR BABY IS BORN

We prepared for our baby by attending Expectant Parent Classes:

___yes ___no

Labor began on _____ at ___ o'clock.

I went to the hospital at ___ o'clock. Name and location of hospital_____
_____

Husband (or a significant other) was with me during labor:

___yes ___no   Labor lasted ___ hours, delivery ___ hours.

Our baby was born (date) _____ at ___ o'clock.

City _____ County _____ State _____

Attending doctors and nurses _____
_____

I was able to breastfeed and hold my baby during the first hours of life:

___yes ___no

The father was able to hold the baby during the first hours of life:

___yes ___no

Family-centered care was available at my hospital:

___yes ___no

Baby "roomed in":   ___yes ___no

Father took care of baby: ___yes ___no

Siblings visited: ___yes ___no

Additional comments _____
_____
_____
_____

WE PROUDLY PRESENT

Name _____

Named for _____

Religious ceremony _____
_____

Clergyman officiating _____

Godmother _____

Godfather _____

Those present _____
_____
_____

Attach baby's first photograph and birth announcement

IDENTIFICATION MARKS

Attach hospital identification here

| Birthmarks
Location: Make drawings to show shape and size | Palmprints or Footprints |

Color of eyes at birth _____ six mos. _____ nine mos. _____
Color of hair at birth _____ six mos. _____ nine mos. _____
   brows _____
   lashes _____
Complexion _____ Shape of head _____

Birth Certificate

Place a copy of baby's birth certificate on this page. Your local or State Health Department will furnish one on your request. The birth certificate remains valuable throughout life. It provides proof of parents' and child's identities and citizenship; it establishes rights to attend school, hold public office, obtain social security number, get passports, inherit property, etc.; it also assures mother's right to a pension.

BABY'S FIRST YEAR... MENTAL, PHYSICAL, AND SOCIAL DEVELOPMENT

All children go through similar stages of development, but in their own ways and at their own rates. The age classifications given below are approximate. Wide variations occur within normal limits. Fill in the ages at which your child reaches the following typical stages, but do not try to hurry the process. Praise all efforts and accomplishments.

Newborn

_____ All limb movements are reflex responses

One month old

_____ Preferred position (usually lying on back) finds child with head turned toward favored side, with hand extended

Two months old

_____ Responds to voice with symmetrical limb movements and to noises with crying

Three months old

_____ Lifts head up 45 degrees while lying on stomach

Four months old

_____ Eyes now follow moving object

Five months old

_____ Smiles spontaneously at your face

Six months old

_____ Vocal play ("babbling") includes combinations of sounds and some repetition. Shows sensitivity to stern sounds in environment

Seven months old

_____ Maintains sitting position for long periods of time

Eight months old

_____ Withdrawal or crying when a stranger approaches. Indicates the child's ability to distinguish between the familiar and unfamiliar

Nine months old

_____ Begins to crawl (allow plenty of opportunity and space)

Ten months old

_____ Pulls self to standing position. Advanced stages of grasping and manipulating objects

Eleven months old

_____ Uses spoon, if filled for him

Twelve months old

_____ Imitates speech and musical sounds; may be saying first true words

SECOND YEAR GROWTH ... AND DEVELOPMENT

Here's how our child goes to sleep:

We make sleep attractive by use of _____ musical toy _____ stories

Nap times: morning from _____ to _____; afternoon from _____ to _____

Night sleep approximately from _____ to _____, average of _____ hours daily

Takes favorite toy or blanket _____

Health habits:

Brushes teeth _____ with help _____ by self How many teeth? _____

Handwashing after elimination at age _____

Handwashing before meals at age _____

Daily bath _____

Dressing—starts to help by _____

Physical activity:

Develops body control (insert age):

running_____ jumping_____ exploring_____ pedals kiddie car_____

climbing_____ sliding_____ swinging_____ kicks and throws a ball_____

Here's what he has to say ... and what he means

_____
_____
_____
_____

THIRD YEAR GROWTH...
AND DEVELOPMENT

Favorite foods:

Morning	Noon	Evening	Snacks
_____	_____	_____	_____

Health habits:

Brushes teeth ____with help ____by self ____before breakfast

____after meals ____at bedtime

Elimination (if accidental, do not show disgust)

regular times at ____ and at ____; stays dry during the day at _____

Learning to: **At age of**

Speak in sentences—as tools of thought—says: _____

_____ ____

Give identification (name, address, etc.) ____

Follow simple directions ____

Dressing self:

____selects clothes to wear next day

____helps to dress self ____can undress alone

Increasing motor ability (use of muscles not well controlled): **At age of**

Walks up steps—jumps down ____

Opens door ____

Climbs ladder to slide ____

Pedals a tricycle ____

Develops new speech sounds ____

OUR BABY IS BORN

We prepared for our baby by attending Expectant Parent Classes:

____yes ____no

Labor began on _____ at ____ o'clock.

I went to the hospital at ____ o'clock. Name and location of hospital_____
_____

Husband (or a significant other) was with me during labor:

____yes ____no   Labor lasted ____ hours, delivery ____ hours.

Our baby was born (date) _____ at ____ o'clock.

City _____ County _____ State _____

Attending doctors and nurses _____
_____

I was able to breastfeed and hold my baby during the first hours of life:

____yes ____no

The father was able to hold the baby during the first hours of life:

____yes ____no

Family-centered care was available at my hospital:

____yes ____no

Baby "roomed in":   ____yes ____no

Father took care of baby: ____yes ____no

Siblings visited: ____yes ____no

Additional comments _____
_____
_____
_____
_____

WE PROUDLY PRESENT

Name _____

Named for _____

Religious ceremony _____
_____

Clergyman officiating _____

Godmother _____

Godfather _____

Those present _____
_____
_____

Attach baby's first photograph and birth announcement

IDENTIFICATION MARKS

Attach hospital identification here

| Birthmarks
Location: Make drawings to show shape and size | Palmprints or Footprints |

Color of eyes at birth _____ six mos. _____ nine mos. _____

Color of hair at birth _____ six mos. _____ nine mos. _____

    brows _____

    lashes _____

Complexion _____ Shape of head _____

Birth Certificate

Place a copy of baby's birth certificate on this page. Your local or State Health Department will furnish one on your request. The birth certificate remains valuable throughout life. It provides proof of parents' and child's identities and citizenship; it establishes rights to attend school, hold public office, obtain social security number, get passports, inherit property, etc.; it also assures mother's right to a pension.

BABY'S FIRST YEAR ... MENTAL, PHYSICAL, AND SOCIAL DEVELOPMENT

All children go through similar stages of development, but in their own ways and at their own rates. The age classifications given below are approximate. Wide variations occur within normal limits. Fill in the ages at which your child reaches the following typical stages, but do not try to hurry the process. Praise all efforts and accomplishments.

Newborn

_____ All limb movements are reflex responses

One month old

_____ Preferred position (usually lying on back) finds child with head turned toward favored side, with hand extended

Two months old

_____ Responds to voice with symmetrical limb movements and to noises with crying

Three months old

_____ Lifts head up 45 degrees while lying on stomach

Four months old

_____ Eyes now follow moving object

Five months old

_____ Smiles spontaneously at your face

Six months old

_____ Vocal play ("babbling") includes combinations of sounds and some repetition. Shows sensitivity to stern sounds in environment

Seven months old

_____ Maintains sitting position for long periods of time

Eight months old

_____ Withdrawal or crying when a stranger approaches. Indicates the child's ability to distinguish between the familiar and unfamiliar

Nine months old

_____ Begins to crawl (allow plenty of opportunity and space)

Ten months old

_____ Pulls self to standing position. Advanced stages of grasping and manipulating objects

Eleven months old

_____ Uses spoon, if filled for him

Twelve months old

_____ Imitates speech and musical sounds; may be saying first true words

SECOND YEAR GROWTH...
AND DEVELOPMENT

Here's how our child goes to sleep:

    We make sleep attractive by use of   ____musical toy   ____stories

    Nap times: morning from ____ to ____;   afternoon from ____ to ____

    Night sleep approximately from ____ to ____, average of ____ hours daily

    Takes favorite toy or blanket _____

Health habits:

    Brushes teeth   ____with help   ____by self   How many teeth? ____

    Handwashing after elimination at age ____

    Handwashing before meals at age ____

    Daily bath _____

Dressing—starts to help by _____

Physical activity:

    Develops body control (insert age):

        running____   jumping____   exploring____   pedals kiddie car____

        climbing____   sliding____   swinging____   kicks and throws a ball____

Here's what he has to say . . . and what he means

_____

_____

_____

_____

THIRD YEAR GROWTH...
AND DEVELOPMENT

Favorite foods:

Morning	Noon	Evening	Snacks
_____	_____	_____	_____

Health habits:

Brushes teeth ____with help ____by self ____before breakfast ____after meals ____at bedtime

Elimination (if accidental, do not show disgust)

regular times at ____ and at ____; stays dry during the day at _____

Learning to: **At age of**

Speak in sentences—as tools of thought—says: _____
_____ ____

Give identification (name, address, etc.) ____

Follow simple directions ____

Dressing self:

____selects clothes to wear next day

____helps to dress self   ____can undress alone

Increasing motor ability (use of muscles not well controlled): **At age of**

Walks up steps—jumps down ____

Opens door ____

Climbs ladder to slide ____

Pedals a tricycle ____

Develops new speech sounds ____

FAMILY HEALTH

YOUR COMPLETE RECORD

PRENATAL CARE

Date	Description (problem, medication, doctor visits, etc.)	Follow-up

PRENATAL CARE

Date	Description (problem, medication, doctor visits, etc.)	Follow-up

FAMILY MEDICAL BACKGROUND

Any disease that "runs in your family" should be discussed with your doctor. But first you need this record.

	Father	Pat. Grndfr. 6/29/19	Pat. Grndmr. 1/28/23	Mother 7/20/40	Mat. Grndfr.	Mat. Grndmr.	Siblings		Spouse	Children		
Allergies												
Amblyopia (lazy eye)												
Anemia												
Asthma												
Arthritis	✓		✓									
Bladder/kidney trouble												
Bleeding tendencies												
Cancer or tumor												
Diabetes												
Epilepsy												
Glaucoma												
Gout												
Hearing defects												
Heart trouble	✓											
High blood pressure				✓								
Mental illness												
Mental retardation												
Rheumatism												
Stomach/duodenal ulcer												
Strabismus (crossed eyes)												
Stroke			✓									
Tuberculosis												
Other												
Age at death		54	70									
Gen. health (good, poor)	G											
Birthdate	7/12/40											

136

FAMILY MEDICAL BACKGROUND

Any disease that "runs in your family" should be discussed with your doctor. But first you need this record.

	Father	Pat. Grndfr.	Pat. Grndmr.	Mother	Mat. Grndfr.	Mat. Grndmr.	Siblings		Spouse	Children	
Allergies											
Amblyopia (lazy eye)											
Anemia											
Asthma											
Arthritis											
Bladder/kidney trouble											
Bleeding tendencies											
Cancer or tumor											
Diabetes											
Epilepsy											
Glaucoma											
Gout											
Hearing defects											
Heart trouble											
High blood pressure											
Mental illness											
Mental retardation											
Rheumatism											
Stomach/duodenal ulcer											
Strabismus (crossed eyes)											
Stroke											
Tuberculosis											
Other											
Age at death											
Gen. health (good, poor)											
Birthdate											

FAMILY MEDICAL BACKGROUND

Additional Information

BLOOD GROUP, DONATIONS

Name Robert J. ARNOLD

The blood group should be recorded. It remains the same throughout life.

Blood type B   Rh factor: ✓ Positive   ___ Negative

RECORD OF BLOOD DONATIONS

Date	Blood Bank	Address

BLOOD GROUP, DONATIONS

Name CAROL F. ARNOLD

The blood group should be recorded. It remains the same throughout life.

Blood type _____   Rh factor: __✓__ Positive   _____ Negative

RECORD OF BLOOD DONATIONS

Date	Blood Bank	Address

BLOOD GROUP, DONATIONS

Name _____

The blood group should be recorded. It remains the same throughout life.

Blood type _____   Rh factor: ____ Positive   ____ Negative

RECORD OF BLOOD DONATIONS

Date	Blood Bank	Address

BLOOD GROUP, DONATIONS

Name _____

The blood group should be recorded. It remains the same throughout life.

Blood type _____   Rh factor: ____ Positive   ____ Negative

RECORD OF BLOOD DONATIONS

Date　　　　　　**Blood Bank**　　　　　　　　　　　**Address**

____ _____ _____

____ _____ _____

____ _____ _____

____ _____ _____

____ _____ _____

____ _____ _____

____ _____ _____

____ _____ _____

____ _____ _____

____ _____ _____

____ _____ _____

____ _____ _____

BLOOD GROUP, DONATIONS

Name _____

The blood group should be recorded. It remains the same throughout life.

Blood type _____   Rh factor: ___ Positive   ___ Negative

RECORD OF BLOOD DONATIONS

Date	Blood Bank	Address

BLOOD GROUP, DONATIONS

Name _____

The blood group should be recorded. It remains the same throughout life.

Blood type _____   Rh factor: ____ Positive   ____ Negative

RECORD OF BLOOD DONATIONS

Date   **Blood Bank**   **Address**

RECORD OF BLOOD TRANSFUSIONS RECEIVED

Name _____

Date _____ Doctor _____

Hospital _____

Number of units received _____

Remarks _____

Name _____

Date _____ Doctor _____

Hospital _____

Number of units received _____

Remarks _____

Name _____

Date _____ Doctor _____

Hospital _____

Number of units received _____

Remarks _____

Name _____

Date _____ Doctor _____

Hospital _____

Number of units received _____

Remarks _____

THE NEWBORN'S IMMUNIZATION SCHEDULE

The American Academy of Pediatrics' recommended schedule for active immunization of normal infants and children is below. This constitutes a good preliminary guide as to childhood immunization practices; but these may be modified from year to year, and regular medical contact is advised to remain current.

2 months	DTP	(Diphtheria and tetanus combined with pertusis [whooping cough] vaccine)
4 months	DTP Polio	
6 months	DTP	
1 year	Tuberculin test	
15 months	Rubeola (old-fashioned measles) vaccine Rubella (German measles) vaccine Mumps	
1½ years	DTP Polio	
4–6 years	DTP Polio	
14–16 years	Combined tetanus and diphtheria; repeat every 10 years	

Tetanus toxoid at time of injury: For clean, minor wounds, no booster dose is needed by a fully immunized child unless more than 10 years have elapsed since the last dose. For contaminated wounds, a booster dose should be given if more than 5 years have elapsed since the last dose.

IMMUNIZATIONS: A LIFE RECORD

Family Member _____

Type of Shot	Physician	Date
_____	_____	_____
_____	_____	_____
_____	_____	_____
_____	_____	_____
_____	_____	_____
_____	_____	_____
_____	_____	_____
_____	_____	_____
_____	_____	_____
_____	_____	_____
_____	_____	_____
_____	_____	_____
_____	_____	_____
_____	_____	_____
_____	_____	_____

IMMUNIZATIONS: A LIFE RECORD

Family Member _____

Type of Shot	Physician	Date

IMMUNIZATIONS: A LIFE RECORD

Family Member _____

Type of Shot	Physician	Date

IMMUNIZATIONS: A LIFE RECORD

Family Member _____

Type of Shot	Physician	Date

IMMUNIZATIONS: A LIFE RECORD

Family Member _____

Type of Shot	Physician	Date

IMMUNIZATIONS: A LIFE RECORD

Family Member _____

Type of Shot	Physician	Date
_____	_____	_____
_____	_____	_____
_____	_____	_____
_____	_____	_____
_____	_____	_____
_____	_____	_____
_____	_____	_____
_____	_____	_____
_____	_____	_____
_____	_____	_____
_____	_____	_____
_____	_____	_____
_____	_____	_____
_____	_____	_____

ADULT WEIGHT RECORD

Family member _____

Date	Weight	Age	Date	Weight	Age
____	_____	___	____	_____	___
____	_____	___	____	_____	___
____	_____	___	____	_____	___
____	_____	___	____	_____	___
____	_____	___	____	_____	___
____	_____	___	____	_____	___
____	_____	___	____	_____	___
____	_____	___	____	_____	___
____	_____	___	____	_____	___
____	_____	___	____	_____	___
____	_____	___	____	_____	___
____	_____	___	____	_____	___
____	_____	___	____	_____	___
____	_____	___	____	_____	___

ADULT WEIGHT RECORD

Family member _____

Date	Weight	Age	Date	Weight	Age
_____	_____	_____	_____	_____	_____
_____	_____	_____	_____	_____	_____
_____	_____	_____	_____	_____	_____
_____	_____	_____	_____	_____	_____
_____	_____	_____	_____	_____	_____
_____	_____	_____	_____	_____	_____
_____	_____	_____	_____	_____	_____
_____	_____	_____	_____	_____	_____
_____	_____	_____	_____	_____	_____
_____	_____	_____	_____	_____	_____
_____	_____	_____	_____	_____	_____
_____	_____	_____	_____	_____	_____
_____	_____	_____	_____	_____	_____
_____	_____	_____	_____	_____	_____

ADULT WEIGHT RECORD

Family member _____

Date	Weight	Age	Date	Weight	Age
____	_____	___	____	_____	___
____	_____	___	____	_____	___
____	_____	___	____	_____	___
____	_____	___	____	_____	___
____	_____	___	____	_____	___
____	_____	___	____	_____	___
____	_____	___	____	_____	___
____	_____	___	____	_____	___
____	_____	___	____	_____	___
____	_____	___	____	_____	___
____	_____	___	____	_____	___
____	_____	___	____	_____	___
____	_____	___	____	_____	___
____	_____	___	____	_____	___
____	_____	___	____	_____	___
____	_____	___	____	_____	___

ADULT WEIGHT RECORD

Family member _____

Date	Weight	Age	Date	Weight	Age
____	____	____	____	____	____
____	____	____	____	____	____
____	____	____	____	____	____
____	____	____	____	____	____
____	____	____	____	____	____
____	____	____	____	____	____
____	____	____	____	____	____
____	____	____	____	____	____
____	____	____	____	____	____
____	____	____	____	____	____
____	____	____	____	____	____
____	____	____	____	____	____
____	____	____	____	____	____
____	____	____	____	____	____

ADULT WEIGHT RECORD

Family member _____

Date	Weight	Age	Date	Weight	Age
____	____	____	____	____	____
____	____	____	____	____	____
____	____	____	____	____	____
____	____	____	____	____	____
____	____	____	____	____	____
____	____	____	____	____	____
____	____	____	____	____	____
____	____	____	____	____	____
____	____	____	____	____	____
____	____	____	____	____	____
____	____	____	____	____	____
____	____	____	____	____	____
____	____	____	____	____	____
____	____	____	____	____	____
____	____	____	____	____	____
____	____	____	____	____	____

ADULT WEIGHT RECORD

Family member _____

Date	Weight	Age	Date	Weight	Age
____	_____	___	____	_____	___
____	_____	___	____	_____	___
____	_____	___	____	_____	___
____	_____	___	____	_____	___
____	_____	___	____	_____	___
____	_____	___	____	_____	___
____	_____	___	____	_____	___
____	_____	___	____	_____	___
____	_____	___	____	_____	___
____	_____	___	____	_____	___
____	_____	___	____	_____	___
____	_____	___	____	_____	___
____	_____	___	____	_____	___
____	_____	___	____	_____	___

CONTAGIOUS DISEASE RECORDS

Family Member _____

CHICKENPOX

Onset date _____

Duration _____

Doctor _____

Address _____

Treatment _____

Remarks _____

HEPATITIS

Onset date _____

Duration _____

Doctor _____

Address _____

Treatment _____

Remarks _____

MONONUCLEOSIS (GLANDULAR FEVER)

Onset date _____

Duration _____

Doctor _____

Address _____

Treatment _____

Remarks _____

CONTAGIOUS DISEASE RECORDS (cont'd)

MUMPS

Onset date _____

Duration _____

Doctor _____

Address _____

Treatment _____

Remarks _____

POLIO

Onset date _____

Duration _____

Doctor _____

Address _____

Treatment _____

Remarks _____

RUBEOLA
(OLD-FASHIONED MEASLES) (REGULAR MEASLES)

Onset date _____

Duration _____

Doctor _____

Address _____

Treatment _____

Remarks _____

CONTAGIOUS DISEASE RECORDS (cont'd)

RUBELLA
(GERMAN MEASLES) (THREE-DAY MEASLES)

Onset date _____

Duration _____

Doctor _____

Address _____

Treatment _____

Remarks _____

SCARLET FEVER

Onset date _____

Duration _____

Doctor _____

Address _____

Treatment _____

Remarks _____

WHOOPING COUGH

Onset date _____

Duration _____

Doctor _____

Address _____

Treatment _____

Remarks _____

CONTAGIOUS DISEASE RECORDS (cont'd)

OTHER CONTAGIOUS DISEASES:

_____

Onset date _____

Duration _____

Doctor _____

Address _____

Treatment _____

Remarks _____

_____

Onset date _____

Duration _____

Doctor _____

Address _____

Treatment _____

Remarks _____

_____

Onset date _____

Duration _____

Doctor _____

Address _____

Treatment _____

Remarks _____

CONTAGIOUS DISEASE RECORDS

Family Member _____

CHICKENPOX

Onset date _____

Duration _____

Doctor _____

Address _____

Treatment _____

Remarks _____

HEPATITIS

Onset date _____

Duration _____

Doctor _____

Address _____

Treatment _____

Remarks _____

MONONUCLEOSIS (GLANDULAR FEVER)

Onset date _____

Duration _____

Doctor _____

Address _____

Treatment _____

Remarks _____

CONTAGIOUS DISEASE RECORDS (cont'd)

MUMPS

Onset date _____

Duration _____

Doctor _____

Address _____

Treatment _____

Remarks _____

POLIO

Onset date _____

Duration _____

Doctor _____

Address _____

Treatment _____

Remarks _____

RUBEOLA
(OLD-FASHIONED MEASLES) (REGULAR MEASLES)

Onset date _____

Duration _____

Doctor _____

Address _____

Treatment _____

Remarks _____

CONTAGIOUS DISEASE RECORDS (cont'd)

RUBELLA
(GERMAN MEASLES) (THREE-DAY MEASLES)

Onset date _____

Duration _____

Doctor _____

Address _____

Treatment _____

Remarks _____

SCARLET FEVER

Onset date _____

Duration _____

Doctor _____

Address _____

Treatment _____

Remarks _____

WHOOPING COUGH

Onset date _____

Duration _____

Doctor _____

Address _____

Treatment _____

Remarks _____

CONTAGIOUS DISEASE RECORDS (cont'd)

OTHER CONTAGIOUS DISEASES:

_____

Onset date _____

Duration _____

Doctor _____

Address _____

Treatment _____

Remarks _____

_____

Onset date _____

Duration _____

Doctor _____

Address _____

Treatment _____

Remarks _____

_____

Onset date _____

Duration _____

Doctor _____

Address _____

Treatment _____

Remarks _____

CONTAGIOUS DISEASE RECORDS

Family Member _____

CHICKENPOX

Onset date _____

Duration _____

Doctor _____

Address _____

Treatment _____

Remarks _____

HEPATITIS

Onset date _____

Duration _____

Doctor _____

Address _____

Treatment _____

Remarks _____

MONONUCLEOSIS (GLANDULAR FEVER)

Onset date _____

Duration _____

Doctor _____

Address _____

Treatment _____

Remarks _____

CONTAGIOUS DISEASE RECORDS (cont'd)

MUMPS

Onset date _____

Duration _____

Doctor _____

Address _____

Treatment _____

Remarks _____

POLIO

Onset date _____

Duration _____

Doctor _____

Address _____

Treatment _____

Remarks _____

RUBEOLA
(OLD-FASHIONED MEASLES) (REGULAR MEASLES)

Onset date _____

Duration _____

Doctor _____

Address _____

Treatment _____

Remarks _____

CONTAGIOUS DISEASE RECORDS (cont'd)

FAMILY HISTORY

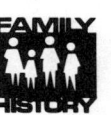

RUBELLA
(GERMAN MEASLES) (THREE-DAY MEASLES)

Onset date ______________________

Duration ______________________

Doctor ______________________

Address ______________________

Treatment ______________________

Remarks ______________________

SCARLET FEVER

Onset date ______________________

Duration ______________________

Doctor ______________________

Address ______________________

Treatment ______________________

Remarks ______________________

WHOOPING COUGH

Onset date ______________________

Duration ______________________

Doctor ______________________

Address ______________________

Treatment ______________________

Remarks ______________________

CONTAGIOUS DISEASE RECORDS (cont'd)

OTHER CONTAGIOUS DISEASES:

_____

Onset date _____

Duration _____

Doctor _____

Address _____

Treatment _____

Remarks _____

_____

Onset date _____

Duration _____

Doctor _____

Address _____

Treatment _____

Remarks _____

_____

Onset date _____

Duration _____

Doctor _____

Address _____

Treatment _____

Remarks _____

CONTAGIOUS DISEASE RECORDS

Family Member _____

CHICKENPOX

Onset date _____

Duration _____

Doctor _____

Address _____

Treatment _____

Remarks _____

HEPATITIS

Onset date _____

Duration _____

Doctor _____

Address _____

Treatment _____

Remarks _____

MONONUCLEOSIS (GLANDULAR FEVER)

Onset date _____

Duration _____

Doctor _____

Address _____

Treatment _____

Remarks _____

CONTAGIOUS DISEASE RECORDS (cont'd)

MUMPS

Onset date _____

Duration _____

Doctor _____

Address _____

Treatment _____

Remarks _____

POLIO

Onset date _____

Duration _____

Doctor _____

Address _____

Treatment _____

Remarks _____

RUBEOLA
(OLD-FASHIONED MEASLES) (REGULAR MEASLES)

Onset date _____

Duration _____

Doctor _____

Address _____

Treatment _____

Remarks _____

CONTAGIOUS DISEASE RECORDS (cont'd)

RUBELLA
(GERMAN MEASLES) (THREE-DAY MEASLES)

Onset date _____

Duration _____

Doctor _____

Address _____

Treatment _____

Remarks _____

SCARLET FEVER

Onset date _____

Duration _____

Doctor _____

Address _____

Treatment _____

Remarks _____

WHOOPING COUGH

Onset date _____

Duration _____

Doctor _____

Address _____

Treatment _____

Remarks _____

CONTAGIOUS DISEASE RECORDS (cont'd)

OTHER CONTAGIOUS DISEASES:

_____

Onset date _____

Duration _____

Doctor _____

Address _____

Treatment _____

Remarks _____

_____

Onset date _____

Duration _____

Doctor _____

Address _____

Treatment _____

Remarks _____

_____

Onset date _____

Duration _____

Doctor _____

Address _____

Treatment _____

Remarks _____

CONTAGIOUS DISEASE RECORDS

Family Member _____

CHICKENPOX

Onset date _____

Duration _____

Doctor _____

Address _____

Treatment _____

Remarks _____

HEPATITIS

Onset date _____

Duration _____

Doctor _____

Address _____

Treatment _____

Remarks _____

MONONUCLEOSIS (GLANDULAR FEVER)

Onset date _____

Duration _____

Doctor _____

Address _____

Treatment _____

Remarks _____

CONTAGIOUS DISEASE RECORDS (cont'd)

MUMPS

Onset date _____

Duration _____

Doctor _____

Address _____

Treatment _____

Remarks _____

POLIO

Onset date _____

Duration _____

Doctor _____

Address _____

Treatment _____

Remarks _____

RUBEOLA
(OLD-FASHIONED MEASLES) (REGULAR MEASLES)

Onset date _____

Duration _____

Doctor _____

Address _____

Treatment _____

Remarks _____

CONTAGIOUS DISEASE RECORDS (cont'd)

FAMILY HISTORY

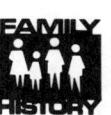

RUBELLA
(GERMAN MEASLES) (THREE-DAY MEASLES)

Onset date ______________________

Duration ______________________

Doctor ______________________

Address ______________________

Treatment ______________________

Remarks ______________________

SCARLET FEVER

Onset date ______________________

Duration ______________________

Doctor ______________________

Address ______________________

Treatment ______________________

Remarks ______________________

WHOOPING COUGH

Onset date ______________________

Duration ______________________

Doctor ______________________

Address ______________________

Treatment ______________________

Remarks ______________________

CONTAGIOUS DISEASE RECORDS (cont'd)

OTHER CONTAGIOUS DISEASES:

_____

Onset date _____

Duration _____

Doctor _____

Address _____

Treatment _____

Remarks _____

_____

Onset date _____

Duration _____

Doctor _____

Address _____

Treatment _____

Remarks _____

_____

Onset date _____

Duration _____

Doctor _____

Address _____

Treatment _____

Remarks _____

CONTAGIOUS DISEASE RECORDS

Family Member _____

CHICKENPOX

Onset date _____

Duration _____

Doctor _____

Address _____

Treatment _____

Remarks _____

HEPATITIS

Onset date _____

Duration _____

Doctor _____

Address _____

Treatment _____

Remarks _____

MONONUCLEOSIS (GLANDULAR FEVER)

Onset date _____

Duration _____

Doctor _____

Address _____

Treatment _____

Remarks _____

CONTAGIOUS DISEASE RECORDS (cont'd)

MUMPS

Onset date _____

Duration _____

Doctor _____

Address _____

Treatment _____

Remarks _____

POLIO

Onset date _____

Duration _____

Doctor _____

Address _____

Treatment _____

Remarks _____

RUBEOLA
(OLD-FASHIONED MEASLES) (REGULAR MEASLES)

Onset date _____

Duration _____

Doctor _____

Address _____

Treatment _____

Remarks _____

CONTAGIOUS DISEASE RECORDS (cont'd)

FAMILY HISTORY

RUBELLA
(GERMAN MEASLES) (THREE-DAY MEASLES)

Onset date ________________________

Duration ________________________

Doctor ________________________

Address ________________________

Treatment ________________________

Remarks ________________________

SCARLET FEVER

Onset date ________________________

Duration ________________________

Doctor ________________________

Address ________________________

Treatment ________________________

Remarks ________________________

WHOOPING COUGH

Onset date ________________________

Duration ________________________

Doctor ________________________

Address ________________________

Treatment ________________________

Remarks ________________________

CONTAGIOUS DISEASE RECORDS (cont'd)

OTHER CONTAGIOUS DISEASES:

_____

Onset date _____

Duration _____

Doctor _____

Address _____

Treatment _____

Remarks _____

_____

Onset date _____

Duration _____

Doctor _____

Address _____

Treatment _____

Remarks _____

_____

Onset date _____

Duration _____

Doctor _____

Address _____

Treatment _____

Remarks _____

MEDICAL ALERT—
FOR EMERGENCY AND REFERENCE USE

Family member _____ Blood type _____

Medical condition _____

Allergic reaction (if any) _____

IN CASE OF EMERGENCY CALL _____

Immediate first-aid information (allergies, contact lenses, epilepsy, etc.) _____
_____
_____

Personal physician _____ Telephone _____

Family member _____ Blood type _____

Medical condition _____

Allergic reaction (if any) _____

IN CASE OF EMERGENCY CALL _____

Immediate first-aid information (allergies, contact lenses, epilepsy, etc.) _____
_____
_____

Personal physician _____ Telephone _____

Family member _____ Blood type _____

Medical condition _____

Allergic reaction (if any) _____

IN CASE OF EMERGENCY CALL _____

Immediate first-aid information (allergies, contact lenses, epilepsy, etc.) _____
_____
_____

Personal physician _____ Telephone _____

MEDICAL ALERT—
FOR EMERGENCY AND REFERENCE USE

Family member _____ Blood type _____

Medical condition _____

Allergic reaction (if any) _____

IN CASE OF EMERGENCY CALL _____

Immediate first-aid information (allergies, contact lenses, epilepsy, etc.) _____
_____
_____

Personal physician _____ Telephone _____

Family member _____ Blood type _____

Medical condition _____

Allergic reaction (if any) _____

IN CASE OF EMERGENCY CALL _____

Immediate first-aid information (allergies, contact lenses, epilepsy, etc.) _____
_____
_____

Personal physician _____ Telephone _____

Family member _____ Blood type _____

Medical condition _____

Allergic reaction (if any) _____

IN CASE OF EMERGENCY CALL _____

Immediate first-aid information (allergies, contact lenses, epilepsy, etc.) _____
_____
_____

Personal physician _____ Telephone _____

HEALTH EXAMINATIONS

Family Member	Date	Doctor	Type of Examination/Results	Doctor's Recommendations

HEALTH EXAMINATIONS

Family Member	Date	Doctor	Type of Examination/Results	Doctor's Recommendations

MAJOR LABORATORY EXAMINATIONS

FAMILY HISTORY

Name _____

Date _____ Referring physician _____

Laboratory _____

Address _____

Type of test(s) _____

Results _____

Name _____

Date _____ Referring physician _____

Laboratory _____

Address _____

Type of test(s) _____

Results _____

Name _____

Date _____ Referring physician _____

Laboratory _____

Address _____

Type of test(s) _____

Results _____

Name _____

Date _____ Referring physician _____

Laboratory _____

Address _____

Type of test(s) _____

Results _____

MAJOR LABORATORY EXAMINATIONS

Name _____

Date _____ Referring physician _____

Laboratory _____

Address _____

Type of test(s) _____

Results _____

Name _____

Date _____ Referring physician _____

Laboratory _____

Address _____

Type of test(s) _____

Results _____

Name _____

Date _____ Referring physician _____

Laboratory _____

Address _____

Type of test(s) _____

Results _____

Name _____

Date _____ Referring physician _____

Laboratory _____

Address _____

Type of test(s) _____

Results _____

ELECTROCARDIOGRAMS

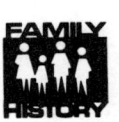

FAMILY HISTORY

Name ______________________________

Date __________ Referring physician ______________________________

Hospital or clinic ______________________________

Address ______________________________

Results ______________________________

____

Name ______________________________

Date __________ Referring physician ______________________________

Hospital or clinic ______________________________

Address ______________________________

Results ______________________________

____

Name ______________________________

Date __________ Referring physician ______________________________

Hospital or clinic ______________________________

Address ______________________________

Results ______________________________

____

Name ______________________________

Date __________ Referring physician ______________________________

Hospital or clinic ______________________________

Address ______________________________

Results ______________________________

____

ELECTROCARDIOGRAMS

Name _____

Date _____ Referring physician _____

Hospital or clinic _____

Address _____

Results _____

_____

Name _____

Date _____ Referring physician _____

Hospital or clinic _____

Address _____

Results _____

_____

Name _____

Date _____ Referring physician _____

Hospital or clinic _____

Address _____

Results _____

_____

Name _____

Date _____ Referring physician _____

Hospital or clinic _____

Address _____

Results _____

_____

HOSPITAL ADMISSIONS

Family member _____

Admission date _____

Reason(s) _____

_____

Doctor(s) _____

_____

Hospital _____

_____

Treatment _____

_____

_____

Costs _____

_____

Insurance coverage _____

_____

Discharge date _____

HOSPITAL ADMISSIONS

Family member _____

Admission date _____

Reason(s) _____

_____

Doctor(s) _____

_____

Hospital _____

_____

Treatment _____

_____

_____

Costs _____

_____

Insurance coverage _____

_____

Discharge date _____

HOSPITAL ADMISSIONS

FAMILY HISTORY

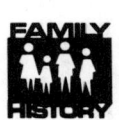

Family member ______________________________

Admission date ______________________________

Reason(s) ______________________________

____

Doctor(s) ______________________________

____

Hospital ______________________________

____

Treatment ______________________________

____

____

Costs ______________________________

____

Insurance coverage ______________________________

____

Discharge date ______________________________

HOSPITAL ADMISSIONS

Family member _____

Admission date _____

Reason(s) _____
_____

Doctor(s) _____
_____

Hospital _____
_____

Treatment _____
_____
_____

Costs _____
_____

Insurance coverage _____
_____

Discharge date _____

ACUTE ILLNESSES

UNSCHEDULED VISITS TO A PHYSICIAN

Keep records of illnesses having a rapid onset, *severe symptoms,* and running a short course, other than contagious diseases, those requiring hospitalization, or injury.

Family member _____

Illness _____

Onset date _____ Duration _____

Doctor _____

Address _____

Treatment _____

_____

_____

Discharge date _____

Family member _____

Illness _____

Onset date _____ Duration _____

Doctor _____

Address _____

Treatment _____

_____

_____

Discharge date _____

ACUTE ILLNESSES (cont'd)

UNSCHEDULED VISITS TO A PHYSICIAN

Family member _____

Illness _____

Onset date _____ Duration _____

Doctor _____

Address _____

Treatment _____

_____

_____

_____

Discharge date _____

Family member _____

Illness _____

Onset date _____ Duration _____

Doctor _____

Address _____

Treatment _____

_____

_____

_____

Discharge date _____

ACUTE ILLNESSES (cont'd)

FAMILY HISTORY

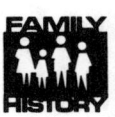

UNSCHEDULED VISITS TO A PHYSICIAN

Family member ______________________________

Illness ______________________________

Onset date __________ Duration ______________________________

Doctor ______________________________

Address ______________________________

Treatment ______________________________

____

____

____

Discharge date ______________________________

Family member ______________________________

Illness ______________________________

Onset date __________ Duration ______________________________

Doctor ______________________________

Address ______________________________

Treatment ______________________________

____

____

____

Discharge date ______________________________

ACCIDENTS

Family member _____

Date _____ Injury _____

Place of accident _____

Doctor _____

Place where treated _____

Treatment and remarks _____

_____

Family member _____

Date _____ Injury _____

Place of accident _____

Doctor _____

Place where treated _____

Treatment and remarks _____

_____

Family member _____

Date _____ Injury _____

Place of accident _____

Doctor _____

Place where treated _____

Treatment and remarks _____

_____

ACCIDENTS

Family member _____

Date _____ Injury _____

Place of accident _____

Doctor _____

Place where treated _____

Treatment and remarks _____

_____

Family member _____

Date _____ Injury _____

Place of accident _____

Doctor _____

Place where treated _____

Treatment and remarks _____

_____

Family member _____

Date _____ Injury _____

Place of accident _____

Doctor _____

Place where treated _____

Treatment and remarks _____

_____

OPTICAL HISTORY

Family Member	Date	Doctor	Prescriptions/Medications

OPTICAL HISTORY

Family Member	Date	Doctor	Prescriptions/Medications

DENTAL HISTORY

Family Member	Date	Dentist	Treatment, Medication, X rays, and Diagnosis

DENTAL HISTORY

Family Member	Date	Dentist	Treatment, Medication, X rays, and Diagnosis

X-RAY HISTORIES

Family Member	Date	Purpose/Kind	Where Taken	Where Stored

X-RAY HISTORIES

Family Member	Date	Purpose/Kind	Where Taken	Where Stored

PRESCRIBED MEDICATIONS

Record only medicines that are taken regularly.

Family member _____

Name of medicine _____

Doctor _____

Date (from-to) _____ Prescription no. _____

Pharmacy _____

Reason for taking _____
_____

Family member _____

Name of medicine _____

Doctor _____

Date (from-to) _____ Prescription no. _____

Pharmacy _____

Reason for taking _____
_____

Family member _____

Name of medicine _____

Doctor _____

Date (from-to) _____ Prescription no. _____

Pharmacy _____

Reason for taking _____
_____

PRESCRIBED MEDICATIONS (cont'd)

Family member _____

Name of medicine _____

Doctor _____

Date (from-to) _____ Prescription no. _____

Pharmacy _____

Reason for taking _____

_____

Family member _____

Name of medicine _____

Doctor _____

Date (from-to) _____ Prescription no. _____

Pharmacy _____

Reason for taking _____

_____

Family member _____

Name of medicine _____

Doctor _____

Date (from-to) _____ Prescription no. _____

Pharmacy _____

Reason for taking _____

_____

ADVERSE REACTIONS TO PRESCRIBED MEDICATION

Family member _____

Name of medicine _____

Doctor and address _____
_____

Reason for taking _____

Date of reaction _____

Reaction _____

Family member _____

Name of medicine _____

Doctor and address _____
_____

Reason for taking _____

Date of reaction _____

Reaction _____

Family member _____

Name of medicine _____

Doctor and address _____
_____

Reason for taking _____

Date of reaction _____

Reaction _____

ADVERSE REACTIONS TO PRESCRIBED MEDICATION

Family member _____

Name of medicine _____

Doctor and address _____

_____

Reason for taking _____

Date of reaction _____

Reaction _____

Family member _____

Name of medicine _____

Doctor and address _____

_____

Reason for taking _____

Date of reaction _____

Reaction _____

Family member _____

Name of medicine _____

Doctor and address _____

_____

Reason for taking _____

Date of reaction _____

Reaction _____

ADDITIONAL HEALTH RECORDS

Family member _____

Medical problem _____

Doctor _____

Address _____

Treatment _____

Prescriptions, examinations _____

_____

_____

Recommendations _____

_____

_____

Family member _____

Medical problem _____

Doctor _____

Address _____

Treatment _____

Prescriptions, examinations _____

_____

_____

Recommendations _____

_____

_____

ADDITIONAL HEALTH RECORDS

Family member _____

Medical problem _____

Doctor _____

Address _____

Treatment _____

Prescriptions, examinations _____

_____

_____

Recommendations _____

_____

_____

Family member _____

Medical problem _____

Doctor _____

Address _____

Treatment _____

Prescriptions, examinations _____

_____

_____

Recommendations _____

_____

_____

UNTIL DEATH US DO PART

WEDDING GIFTS

Gift	Date Rec'd	From	Thank-you Sent
_____	_____	_____	_____
_____	_____	_____	_____
_____	_____	_____	_____
_____	_____	_____	_____
_____	_____	_____	_____
_____	_____	_____	_____
_____	_____	_____	_____
_____	_____	_____	_____
_____	_____	_____	_____
_____	_____	_____	_____
_____	_____	_____	_____
_____	_____	_____	_____
_____	_____	_____	_____
_____	_____	_____	_____
_____	_____	_____	_____
_____	_____	_____	_____

WEDDING GIFTS

Gift	Date Rec'd	From	Thank-you Sent

WEDDING GIFTS

Gift	Date Rec'd	From	Thank-you Sent

SAMPLE APARTMENT-SHARING CONTRACT

_____ and _____ hereby agree that:

1. They will share Apartment _____ at _____ , and will be responsible for its monthly rent of $_____ in this manner:

   _____ – $_____

   _____ – $_____

2. All other communal expenses (food, utilities, etc.) will be shared, with _____ paying ___ percent and _____ paying ___ percent.

3. They further agree that _____ will be responsible for the following duties:

   Food shopping

   Cooking

   Laundry

4. All house cleaning and other maintenance will be split equally.

5. Neither will purchase linens, lamps, furniture, etc., without agreement from the other party.

Date_____   Agreed_____

                              Agreed_____

TERMINATION OF MARRIAGE RECORD

ANNULMENT

Effective date _____

Attorneys _____
_____

Records held at _____
_____

Disposition _____
_____
_____

Remarks _____
_____
_____

SEPARATION

Effective date _____

Attorneys _____
_____

Records held at _____
_____

Remarks _____
_____
_____

TERMINATION OF MARRIAGE RECORD (cont'd)

DIVORCE

Effective date _____

Attorneys _____
_____

Records held at _____
_____

Disposition _____
_____
_____

Remarks _____
_____
_____

Effective date _____

Attorneys _____
_____

Records held at _____
_____

Disposition _____
_____
_____

Remarks _____
_____
_____

INSURANCE

HEALTH, VEHICLE, LIFE, HOMEOWNER'S OR PROPERTY, MORTGAGE, AND OTHER KINDS

FAMILY AND INDIVIDUAL HOSPITALIZATION AND HEALTH INSURANCE

Family member(s) _____

Company _____ Type _____

Coverage _____ Amt. deductible _____

Policy no. _____

Effective date _____ Expiration date _____

Premium _____

Where policy kept _____

Family member(s) _____

Company _____ Type _____

Coverage _____ Amt. deductible _____

Policy no. _____

Effective date _____ Expiration date _____

Premium _____

Where policy kept _____

Family member(s) _____

Company _____ Type _____

Coverage _____ Amt. deductible _____

Policy no. _____

Effective date _____ Expiration date _____

Premium _____

Where policy kept _____

FAMILY AND INDIVIDUAL HOSPITALIZATION AND HEALTH INSURANCE

Family member(s) _____

Company _____ Type _____

Coverage _____ Amt. deductible _____

Policy no. _____

Effective date _____ Expiration date _____

Premium _____

Where policy kept _____

Family member(s) _____

Company _____ Type _____

Coverage _____ Amt. deductible _____

Policy no. _____

Effective date _____ Expiration date _____

Premium _____

Where policy kept _____

Family member(s) _____

Company _____ Type _____

Coverage _____ Amt. deductible _____

Policy no. _____

Effective date _____ Expiration date _____

Premium _____

Where policy kept _____

FAMILY AND INDIVIDUAL HOSPITALIZATION AND HEALTH INSURANCE

Family member(s) _____

Company _____ Type _____

Coverage _____ Amt. deductible _____

Policy no. _____

Effective date _____ Expiration date _____

Premium _____

Where policy kept _____

Family member(s) _____

Company _____ Type _____

Coverage _____ Amt. deductible _____

Policy no. _____

Effective date _____ Expiration date _____

Premium _____

Where policy kept _____

Family member(s) _____

Company _____ Type _____

Coverage _____ Amt. deductible _____

Policy no. _____

Effective date _____ Expiration date _____

Premium _____

Where policy kept _____

FAMILY AND INDIVIDUAL HOSPITALIZATION AND HEALTH INSURANCE

Family member(s) _____

Company _____ Type _____

Coverage _____ Amt. deductible _____

Policy no. _____

Effective date _____ Expiration date _____

Premium _____

Where policy kept _____

Family member(s) _____

Company _____ Type _____

Coverage _____ Amt. deductible _____

Policy no. _____

Effective date _____ Expiration date _____

Premium _____

Where policy kept _____

Family member(s) _____

Company _____ Type _____

Coverage _____ Amt. deductible _____

Policy no. _____

Effective date _____ Expiration date _____

Premium _____

Where policy kept _____

DISABILITY/INCOME PROTECTION

Family member _____

Compensation _____ Type _____

Policy no. _____

Coverage _____

Where policy kept _____

_____

Family member _____

Compensation _____ Type _____

Policy no. _____

Coverage _____

Where policy kept _____

_____

Family member _____

Compensation _____ Type _____

Policy no. _____

Coverage _____

Where policy kept _____

_____

Family member _____

Compensation _____ Type _____

Policy no. _____

Coverage _____

Where policy kept _____

_____

VEHICLE INSURANCE

Vehicle covered _____ License no. _____

Description of vehicle _____

Date purchased _____ Registration no. _____

Insurance company _____

Agent name _____ Telephone _____

Address _____

Policy no. _____ Renewal date _____

Amount/type of coverage _____

_____

Limitations or exclusions _____

_____

_____

Vehicle covered _____ License no. _____

Description of vehicle _____

Date purchased _____ Registration no. _____

Insurance company _____

Agent name _____ Telephone _____

Address _____

Policy no. _____ Renewal date _____

Amount/type of coverage _____

_____

Limitations or exclusions _____

_____

_____

VEHICLE INSURANCE

Vehicle covered _____ License no. _____

Description of vehicle _____

Date purchased _____ Registration no. _____

Insurance company _____

Agent name _____ Telephone _____

Address _____

Policy no. _____ Renewal date _____

Amount/type of coverage _____

_____

Limitations or exclusions _____

_____

_____

Vehicle covered _____ License no. _____

Description of vehicle _____

Date purchased _____ Registration no. _____

Insurance company _____

Agent name _____ Telephone _____

Address _____

Policy no. _____ Renewal date _____

Amount/type of coverage _____

_____

Limitations or exclusions _____

_____

_____

LIFE INSURANCE

Family member _____ Type of policy _____

Policy no. _____ Amount _____

Insurance company _____

Agent name _____ Telephone _____

Address _____
_____

Date policy issued _____

Beneficiary _____

Secondary beneficiary _____

Amount of premium _____ Date due _____

Limitations or exclusions _____
_____
_____
_____
_____
_____

Other remarks _____
_____
_____
_____
_____
_____

LIFE INSURANCE

Family member _____ Type of policy _____

Policy no. _____ Amount _____

Insurance company _____

Agent name _____ Telephone _____

Address _____
_____

Date policy issued _____

Beneficiary _____

Secondary beneficiary _____

Amount of premium _____ Date due _____

Limitations or exclusions _____
_____
_____
_____
_____
_____

Other remarks _____
_____
_____
_____
_____
_____

LIFE INSURANCE

Family member _____ Type of policy _____

Policy no. _____ Amount _____

Insurance company _____

Agent name _____ Telephone _____

Address _____
_____

Date policy issued _____

Beneficiary _____

Secondary beneficiary _____

Amount of premium _____ Date due _____

Limitations or exclusions _____
_____
_____
_____
_____
_____

Other remarks _____
_____
_____
_____
_____
_____

LIFE INSURANCE

Family member _____ Type of policy _____

Policy no. _____ Amount _____

Insurance company _____

Agent name _____ Telephone _____

Address _____
_____

Date policy issued _____

Beneficiary _____

Secondary beneficiary _____

Amount of premium _____ Date due _____

Limitations or exclusions _____
_____
_____
_____
_____
_____

Other remarks _____
_____
_____
_____
_____
_____

THIRD-PARTY LIFE INSURANCE

Includes coverage that is employer-provided, separately purchased or provided through union, professional society, or alumni/alumnae association

Family member insured _____

Company _____ Type _____

Policy no. _____ Face value _____

Beneficiary(s) _____

_____

Effective date _____ Expiration date _____

Premium _____

Where policy kept _____

Family member insured _____

Company _____ Type _____

Policy no. _____ Face value _____

Beneficiary(s) _____

_____

Effective date _____ Expiration date _____

Premium _____

Where policy kept _____

Family member insured _____

Company _____ Type _____

Policy no. _____ Face value _____

Beneficiary(s) _____

_____

Effective date _____ Expiration date _____

Premium _____

Where policy kept _____

THIRD-PARTY LIFE INSURANCE

Family member insured _____

Company _____ Type _____

Policy no. _____ Face value _____

Beneficiary(s) _____

_____

Effective date _____ Expiration date _____

Premium _____

Where policy kept _____

Family member insured _____

Company _____ Type _____

Policy no. _____ Face value _____

Beneficiary(s) _____

_____

Effective date _____ Expiration date _____

Premium _____

Where policy kept _____

Family member insured _____

Company _____ Type _____

Policy no. _____ Face value _____

Beneficiary(s) _____

_____

Effective date _____ Expiration date _____

Premium _____

Where policy kept _____

HOMEOWNER'S OR REAL PROPERTY INSURANCE

Company _____ Type _____

Policy no. _____

Value _____ Amt. deductible _____

Effective date _____ Expiration date _____

Premium _____

Where policy kept _____

Company _____ Type _____

Policy no. _____

Value _____ Amt. deductible _____

Effective date _____ Expiration date _____

Premium _____

Where policy kept _____

Company _____ Type _____

Policy no. _____

Value _____ Amt. deductible _____

Effective date _____ Expiration date _____

Premium _____

Where policy kept _____

HOMEOWNER'S OR REAL PROPERTY INSURANCE

Company _____ Type _____

Policy no. _____

Value _____ Amt. deductible _____

Effective date _____ Expiration date _____

Premium _____

Where policy kept _____

Company _____ Type _____

Policy no. _____

Value _____ Amt. deductible _____

Effective date _____ Expiration date _____

Premium _____

Where policy kept _____

Company _____ Type _____

Policy no. _____

Value _____ Amt. deductible _____

Effective date _____ Expiration date _____

Premium _____

Where policy kept _____

MORTGAGE INSURANCE

Type of policy _____ Policy no. _____

Location of property _____

_____

_____

Insurer _____ Telephone _____

Address _____

_____

_____

Type/amount of coverage _____

_____

Effective date _____ Expiration date _____

Special provisions/coverage _____

_____

_____

_____

_____

Limitations or exclusions _____

_____

_____

_____

_____

MORTGAGE INSURANCE

Type of policy _____ Policy no. _____

Location of property _____
_____
_____

Insurer _____ Telephone _____

Address _____
_____
_____

Type/amount of coverage _____
_____

Effective date _____ Expiration date _____

Special provisions/coverage _____
_____
_____
_____
_____
_____

Limitations or exclusions _____
_____
_____
_____
_____
_____

ENDOWMENT AND ANNUITY INSURANCE

Company _____ Type _____

Policy no. _____ Value _____

Premium _____ Annual ☐ Semi-Annual ☐ Monthly ☐ Quarterly ☐

Option _____

Where policy kept _____

Company _____ Type _____

Policy no. _____ Value _____

Premium _____ Annual ☐ Semi-Annual ☐ Monthly ☐ Quarterly ☐

Option _____

Where policy kept _____

Company _____ Type _____

Policy no. _____ Value _____

Premium _____ Annual ☐ Semi-Annual ☐ Monthly ☐ Quarterly ☐

Option _____

Where policy kept _____

ENDOWMENT AND ANNUITY INSURANCE

Company _____ Type _____

Policy no. _____ Value _____

Premium _____ Annual☐ Semi-Annual☐ Monthly☐ Quarterly☐

Option _____

Where policy kept _____

Company _____ Type _____

Policy no. _____ Value _____

Premium _____ Annual☐ Semi-Annual☐ Monthly☐ Quarterly☐

Option _____

Where policy kept _____

Company _____ Type _____

Policy no. _____ Value _____

Premium _____ Annual☐ Semi-Annual☐ Monthly☐ Quarterly☐

Option _____

Where policy kept _____

PERSONAL PROPERTY INSURANCE

Company _____ Type _____

Policy no. _____

Coverage _____

Value _____ Amt. deductible _____

Effective date _____ Expiration date _____

Premium _____

Where policy kept _____

Company _____ Type _____

Policy no. _____

Coverage _____

Value _____ Amt. deductible _____

Effective date _____ Expiration date _____

Premium _____

Where policy kept _____

Company _____ Type _____

Policy no. _____

Coverage _____

Value _____ Amt. deductible _____

Effective date _____ Expiration date _____

Premium _____

Where policy kept _____

PERSONAL PROPERTY INSURANCE

Company _____ Type _____

Policy no. _____

Coverage _____

Value _____ Amt. deductible _____

Effective date _____ Expiration date _____

Premium _____

Where policy kept _____

Company _____ Type _____

Policy no. _____

Coverage _____

Value _____ Amt. deductible _____

Effective date _____ Expiration date _____

Premium _____

Where policy kept _____

Company _____ Type _____

Policy no. _____

Coverage _____

Value _____ Amt. deductible _____

Effective date _____ Expiration date _____

Premium _____

Where policy kept _____

OTHER POLICIES

Family member _____ Type of policy _____

Insurance company _____

Agent name _____ Telephone _____

Address _____

Date policy issued _____ Policy no. _____

Coverage _____

Amount of premium _____ Date due _____

Limitations or exclusions _____

_____

_____

_____

Family member _____ Type of policy _____

Insurance company _____

Agent name _____ Telephone _____

Address _____

Date policy issued _____ Policy no. _____

Coverage _____

Amount of premium _____ Date due _____

Limitations or exclusions _____

_____

_____

_____

OTHER POLICIES

Family member _____ Type of policy _____

Insurance company _____

Agent name _____ Telephone _____

Address _____

Date policy issued _____ Policy no. _____

Coverage _____

Amount of premium _____ Date due _____

Limitations or exclusions _____

_____

_____

_____

Family member _____ Type of policy _____

Insurance company _____

Agent name _____ Telephone _____

Address _____

Date policy issued _____ Policy no. _____

Coverage _____

Amount of premium _____ Date due _____

Limitations or exclusions _____

_____

_____

_____

BUDGETS AND OTHER CONCERNS

A BETTER FAMILY BUDGET

INCOME

Husband's earnings $ _____

Wife's earnings _____

Other family members' earnings _____

Interest and dividends _____

Rents from property; royalties _____

Profits from business _____

Pension/annuity/disability _____

Social Security _____

Other income _____

Total income $ _____

Deduct state, federal, and local income taxes (estimate from your paycheck stubs, or on the basis of last year's taxes) $ _____

Deduct Social Security taxes (from your paycheck stubs) _____

Other payroll deductions (insurance, payroll savings, garnishments, etc.) _____

Net spendable income $ _____

A BETTER FAMILY BUDGET

Expenses, Fixed	Annual Amount	Monthly Amount	Spent in Jan.	Spent in Feb.	Spent in Mar.	Spent in Apr.	Spent in May	Spent in June
This year's special objective								
Mortgage/rent								
Heat								
Light								
Water								
Telephone								
Garbage								
Insurance								
Life								
Health								
Disability								
Auto								
Homeowner's								
Installment payments								
Interest on notes								
Loan repayments								
Reducing back bills								
School/College								
Dues								
Children's allowance								
Child care/household help								

A BETTER FAMILY BUDGET (cont'd)

Expenses, Fixed	Spent in July	Spent in Aug.	Spent in Sept.	Spent in Oct.	Spent in Nov.	Spent in Dec.	Totals
This year's special objective							
Mortgage/rent							
Heat							
Light							
Water							
Telephone							
Garbage							
Insurance							
Life							
Health							
Disability							
Auto							
Homeowner's							
Installment payments							
Interest on notes							
Loan repayments							
Reducing back bills							
School/College							
Dues							
Children's allowance							
Child care/household help							

A BETTER FAMILY BUDGET (cont'd)

Expenses, Variable	Annual Amount	Monthly Amount	Spent in Jan.	Spent in Feb.	Spent in Mar.	Spent in Apr.	Spent in May	Spent in June
Food								
Clothing								
Savings								
Doctor								
Dentist								
Drugs								
Gasoline								
Entertainment								
Books/magazines								
Repairs/upkeep								
Car								
House								
Appliances								
Cleaning, Personal care								
Church/charities								
Furniture								
Household supplies								
Birthdays/Christmas								
Hobbies								
Vacation								
Liquor								
Walking-around money								
Other								
TOTAL								

A BETTER FAMILY BUDGET (cont'd)

Expenses, Variable	Spent in July	Spent in Aug.	Spent in Sept.	Spent in Oct.	Spent in Nov.	Spent in Dec.	Totals
Food							
Clothing							
Savings							
Doctor							
Dentist							
Drugs							
Gasoline							
Entertainment							
Books/magazines							
Repairs/upkeep							
Car							
House							
Appliances							
Cleaning, Personal care							
Church/charities							
Furniture							
Household supplies							
Birthdays/Christmas							
Hobbies							
Vacation							
Liquor							
Walking-around money							
Other							
TOTAL							

THE BUDGET SUPPLEMENT: A MONTHLY BUYING-FOR-LESS GUIDE

Here's a month-to-month shopping guide to good buys on expensive items.

Your Additions

January:	Stoves, refrigerators, freezers, bicycles, books, dresses, linens
February:	Air-conditioning units, bedding, china, clothes driers, curtains
March:	Woolens, washers/driers, luggage, skates, ski equipment, storm windows
April:	Coats (women's, children's), dresses
May:	Handbags, linens, TV sets, carpets, tablecloths, tires
June:	Building materials, furniture, TV sets
July:	Children's clothes, coats (men's), fuel oil, appliances, stereos
August:	Air-conditioning units, bathing suits, fans, hardware, lamps, paints
September:	Camping equipment, cars (new), furniture, gardening equipment
October:	Bicycles, china, fishing equipment, glassware, school clothes
November:	Cars (used), children's clothes, stoves
December:	Blankets, cars (used), men's clothing

SAVINGS RECORD: PASSBOOK SAVINGS ACCOUNTS

Account, Institution	Registered Owner	Amount	Date Opened/ Purch'd	Maturity

SAVINGS RECORD: U.S. SAVINGS BONDS

Account, Institution	Registered Owner	Amount	Date Opened/ Purch'd	Maturity

SAVINGS RECORD: CERTIFICATES OF DEPOSIT

Account, Institution	Registered Owner	Amount	Date Opened/ Purch'd	Maturity

SAVINGS RECORD: OTHER

Account, Institution	Registered Owner	Amount	Date Opened/ Purch'd	Maturity
_____	_____	_____	_____	_____
_____	_____	_____	_____	_____
_____	_____	_____	_____	_____
_____	_____	_____	_____	_____
_____	_____	_____	_____	_____
_____	_____	_____	_____	_____
_____	_____	_____	_____	_____
_____	_____	_____	_____	_____
_____	_____	_____	_____	_____
_____	_____	_____	_____	_____
_____	_____	_____	_____	_____
_____	_____	_____	_____	_____
_____	_____	_____	_____	_____
_____	_____	_____	_____	_____
_____	_____	_____	_____	_____

A FAMILY MONEY-FLOW TABLE MODEL

Enter amount of receipt or payment.

How much money do you keep in your family or personal savings account(s)? In your checking account(s)? Unless you have a NOW or other form of interest-paying checking account, you may be losing money every month.

To maximize gains, you should channel as much income as possible into the accounts that pay interest . . . and keep as little as possible where you receive no interest. A handy way to do that is to spend a few minutes a day recording the day's receipts and payments. The following model money-flow table, extended to cover an entire month, gives you the simple tool you need. Twelve such tables will carry you through an entire year. Your goal: move money into the non-interest bearing account(s) only when you have to.

Month: _____, 19__	First Day of Month			Last Day of Month
Receipts				
Take-home pay				
Other income				
Total				
Payments				
Mortgage or rent				
Taxes, other than withholding				
Installment debts				
Insurance premiums				
Life				
Auto				
Homeowner's				
Health				
Cash for current expenses				
Other				
Total				

SAFE DEPOSIT BOX

Location of box _____ Box no. _____

Location of key(s) _____ Date started _____

Address _____

Authorized signature(s) _____

_____

Contents (and date) _____

SAFE DEPOSIT BOX

Location of box _____ Box no. _____

Location of key(s) _____ Date started _____

Address _____

Authorized signature(s) _____

_____

Contents (and date) _____

BANK ACCOUNTS

Type _____ Date opened _____

Bank and address _____

_____

In name(s) of _____

Account no. _____ Date closed _____

Type _____ Date opened _____

Bank and address _____

_____

In name(s) of _____

Account no. _____ Date closed _____

Type _____ Date opened _____

Bank and address _____

_____

In name(s) of _____

Account no. _____ Date closed _____

Type _____ Date opened _____

Bank and address _____

_____

In name(s) of _____

Account no. _____ Date closed _____

BANK ACCOUNTS

Type _____ Date opened _____

Bank and address _____

_____

In name(s) of _____

Account no. _____ Date closed _____

Type _____ Date opened _____

Bank and address _____

_____

In name(s) of _____

Account no. _____ Date closed _____

Type _____ Date opened _____

Bank and address _____

_____

In name(s) of _____

Account no. _____ Date closed _____

Type _____ Date opened _____

Bank and address _____

_____

In name(s) of _____

Account no. _____ Date closed _____

CREDIT CARDS
AND CHARGE ACCOUNTS

Family Member	Issued by/ Contact if Lost or for Inquiry into Account	Card Number	Expires	Credit Limit
_____	_____	_____	_____	_____
_____	_____	_____	_____	_____
_____	_____	_____	_____	_____
_____	_____	_____	_____	_____
_____	_____	_____	_____	_____
_____	_____	_____	_____	_____
_____	_____	_____	_____	_____
_____	_____	_____	_____	_____
_____	_____	_____	_____	_____
_____	_____	_____	_____	_____
_____	_____	_____	_____	_____
_____	_____	_____	_____	_____
_____	_____	_____	_____	_____
_____	_____	_____	_____	_____

CREDIT CARDS AND CHARGE ACCOUNTS

Family Member	Issued by/ Contact if Lost or for Inquiry into Account	Card Number	Expires	Credit Limit
_____	_____	_____	_____	_____
_____	_____	_____	_____	_____
_____	_____	_____	_____	_____
_____	_____	_____	_____	_____
_____	_____	_____	_____	_____
_____	_____	_____	_____	_____
_____	_____	_____	_____	_____
_____	_____	_____	_____	_____
_____	_____	_____	_____	_____
_____	_____	_____	_____	_____
_____	_____	_____	_____	_____
_____	_____	_____	_____	_____
_____	_____	_____	_____	_____

CHECK CASHING CARDS

Where issued _____

Address _____

In whose name _____

Date _____ Number _____

Expiration date (if any) _____

Where issued _____

Address _____

In whose name _____

Date _____ Number _____

Expiration date (if any) _____

Where issued _____

Address _____

In whose name _____

Date _____ Number _____

Expiration date (if any) _____

Where issued _____

Address _____

In whose name _____

Date _____ Number _____

Expiration date (if any) _____

OTHER LICENSES, CARDS, ETC.

Name _____

Purpose _____ Number _____

Issued by _____

Expiration date _____

Name _____

Purpose _____ Number _____

Issued by _____

Expiration date _____

Name _____

Purpose _____ Number _____

Issued by _____

Expiration date _____

Name _____

Purpose _____ Number _____

Issued by _____

Expiration date _____

Name _____

Purpose _____ Number _____

Issued by _____

Expiration date _____

PASSPORTS

If you travel abroad repeatedly, or for prolonged periods, you should record your passport number.

Name _____

Passport no. _____

Date issued _____ Expiration date _____

Where kept _____

Foreign address _____

Name _____

Passport no. _____

Date issued _____ Expiration date _____

Where kept _____

Foreign address _____

Name _____

Passport no. _____

Date issued _____ Expiration date _____

Where kept _____

Foreign address _____

Name _____

Passport no. _____

Date issued _____ Expiration date _____

Where kept _____

Foreign address _____

PASSPORTS

Name _____

Passport no. _____

Date issued _____ Expiration date _____

Where kept _____

Foreign address _____

Name _____

Passport no. _____

Date issued _____ Expiration date _____

Where kept _____

Foreign address _____

Name _____

Passport no. _____

Date issued _____ Expiration date _____

Where kept _____

Foreign address _____

Name _____

Passport no. _____

Date issued _____ Expiration date _____

Where kept _____

Foreign address _____

UNION MEMBERSHIPS

Name _____

Name of union _____
_____

Local no. _____ Membership no. _____

Dates of membership (from-to) _____

Membership fees and dues _____

Benefits _____
_____
_____

Reasons for leaving _____
_____
_____

Name _____

Name of union _____
_____

Local no. _____ Membership no. _____

Dates of membership (from-to) _____

Membership fees and dues _____

Benefits _____
_____
_____

Reasons for leaving _____
_____
_____

UNION MEMBERSHIPS

Name _____

Name of union _____
_____

Local no. _____ Membership no. _____

Dates of membership (from-to) _____

Membership fees and dues _____

Benefits _____
_____
_____

Reasons for leaving _____
_____
_____

Name _____

Name of union _____
_____

Local no. _____ Membership no. _____

Dates of membership (from-to) _____

Membership fees and dues _____

Benefits _____
_____
_____

Reasons for leaving _____
_____
_____

WORKMEN'S COMPENSATION CLAIMS

Date of injury _____

Nature of injury _____

Date reported _____ Date of award _____

Insurance company _____

_____

_____

Amount of award _____

Remarks _____

_____

_____

_____

Date of injury _____

Nature of injury _____

Date reported _____ Date of award _____

Insurance company _____

_____

_____

Amount of award _____

Remarks _____

_____

_____

_____

WORKMEN'S COMPENSATION CLAIMS

Date of injury _____

Nature of injury _____

Date reported _____ Date of award _____

Insurance company _____

_____

_____

Amount of award _____

Remarks _____

_____

_____

_____

_____

Date of injury _____

Nature of injury _____

Date reported _____ Date of award _____

Insurance company _____

_____

_____

Amount of award _____

Remarks _____

_____

_____

_____

_____

LOAN HISTORY

Family member _____ Account no. _____

Lender's name/address _____

Loan officer _____ Telephone _____

Date borrowed _____ Date repaid _____

Amount borrowed _____ Rate of interest _____

Length of loan _____ Payments _____

Purpose _____

Collateral _____

Family member _____ Account no. _____

Lender's name/address _____

Loan officer _____ Telephone _____

Date borrowed _____ Date repaid _____

Amount borrowed _____ Rate of interest _____

Length of loan _____ Payments _____

Purpose _____

Collateral _____

Family member _____ Account no. _____

Lender's name/address _____

Loan officer _____ Telephone _____

Date borrowed _____ Date repaid _____

Amount borrowed _____ Rate of interest _____

Length of loan _____ Payments _____

Purpose _____

Collateral _____

LOAN HISTORY

Family member _____ Account no. _____

Lender's name/address _____

Loan officer _____ Telephone _____

Date borrowed _____ Date repaid _____

Amount borrowed _____ Rate of interest _____

Length of loan _____ Payments _____

Purpose _____

Collateral _____

Family member _____ Account no. _____

Lender's name/address _____

Loan officer _____ Telephone _____

Date borrowed _____ Date repaid _____

Amount borrowed _____ Rate of interest _____

Length of loan _____ Payments _____

Purpose _____

Collateral _____

Family member _____ Account no. _____

Lender's name/address _____

Loan officer _____ Telephone _____

Date borrowed _____ Date repaid _____

Amount borrowed _____ Rate of interest _____

Length of loan _____ Payments _____

Purpose _____

Collateral _____

INVESTMENTS: SECURITIES

The following form provides a place where you can list securities owned by you or your spouse. You may want to include such securities as common and preferred stocks, bonds, mutual fund shares, commodities, payroll savings plans, and any others you may own.

Owner	Name and Type of Security	Broker Purch'd Through & Phone	Cert. Nos.	Date/Price of Purchase	Date/Price of Sale	Location of Securities	Broker Sold Through

INVESTMENTS: SECURITIES

Owner	Name and Type of Security	Broker Purch'd Through & Phone	Cert. Nos.	Date/Price of Purchase	Date/Price of Sale	Location of Securities	Broker Sold Through

INVESTMENTS: SPECIAL

Do you own special investments? You should have a record of them. On the following list you may want to include such items as stamp/coin collections, antiques and fine furniture, other "collectibles," livestock or pets, investment interests in art or sports individuals or teams, foreign currency, gold or silver, and so on.

Family Owner	Description of Item/ Investment	Cost of Purchase	Seller/Broker: Address & Phone	Appraiser: Address & Phone; Date & Value	Location of Investment	Location of Document(s)

INVESTMENTS: SPECIAL

Family Owner	Description of Item/ Investment	Cost of Purchase	Seller/Broker: Address & Phone	Appraiser: Address & Phone; Date & Value	Location of Investment	Location of Document(s)

PENSION, PROFIT-SHARING, TAXES, RETIREMENT PLANNING

THINGS TO KNOW ABOUT YOUR PENSION PLAN

A Checklist

- How many more years must I work for my pension to vest in part? _____

- In full? _____

- How much has accrued for my pension account so far? _____

- How large a monthly pension would it provide for me alone? _____

- For me and my spouse? _____

- What is the effect on my pension if I leave work for a short time and then return? _____

- If I'm laid off for a while? _____

- How old do I have to be in order to collect regular retirement benefits? _____

- Early retirement? _____

- If I leave the company, is my pension vested? _____

- How is the pension benefit figured? _____

- Are there any benefits besides the pension check—for example, life insurance, disability, health benefits, etc.? _____

- If I die, is there a benefit for my spouse? _____

- If so, how much? _____

- Is my pension insured by the federal Pension Benefit Guaranty Corporation? _____

- In part or in full? _____

- Must I be a union member at retirement in order to collect? _____

- Is this a "multiemployer" plan, where time worked for various employers counts toward the pension benefit? _____

- What employers and what jobs are included? _____

THINGS TO KNOW ABOUT
YOUR PENSION PLAN (cont'd)

Don't wait until retirement to find out how much, or how little, you have coming from your company or union pension plan! Check this now and every few years in the future.

Additional Information

_____

_____

_____

_____

_____

_____

_____

_____

_____

_____

_____

_____

THE RETIREMENT PLAN—FORM 1

Estimated Retirement Living Expenses

You can approach retirement planning as a two-phase process. In the first phase, you estimate what your expenses will be once you retire. You can list the various categories of expenses according to the entries in the form below—and then add any others you believe you may face. When you reach the "inflation factor" in Item 14, pick a number; you will be guessing, but so will everyone else.

Form 2, which follows Form 1, shows how to set up a retirement "game plan" on the basis of what you established with Form 1.

	Per Month	× 12 =	Per Year
1. Food	_____		_____
2. Medical expenses:			
a. Doctor	_____		_____
b. Dentist	_____		_____
c. Medicines	_____		_____
d. Medical insurance to supplement Medicare	_____		_____
3. Clothing and personal care:			
a. Wife	_____		_____
b. Husband	_____		_____
4. Transportation:			
a. Car payments	_____		_____
b. Gas	_____		_____
c. Insurance	_____		_____
d. License	_____		_____
e. Car maintenance (tires and repairs)	_____		_____
5. Recurring expenses:			
a. Entertainment	_____		_____
b. Travel	_____		_____
c. Hobbies	_____		_____
d. Rent/mortgage	_____		_____
e. Other	_____		_____
6. Gifts and contributions	_____		_____
7. Income taxes (if any)	_____		_____
8. Total annual expenses			$_____
9. Expected years of retirement			×_____
10. Total funds needed during retirement			$_____
11. One-time costs			+_____
12. Total funds needed during retirement			$_____
13. Total years to retirement			_____
14. Inflation factor (estimated as %) × total years to retirement			×_____
15. Total inflated living expenses during retirement			$_____

Dividing #15 by #9 = Annual Retirement Fund Needed; this divided by 12 = Monthly Funds Needed.

THE RETIREMENT PLAN—FORM 2

Your Game Plan

Your retirement game plan, drawn up with the aid of Form 2, will give you a rough idea of what you will have to work with after you have retired. You can then begin to plan sensibly for those golden years on the basis of carefully estimated future needs. Forms 1 and 2 make it possible to calculate outgo and income, and should be used together.

	Per Month	× 12 =	Per Year
1. Social Security:			
a. Husband	_____		_____
b. Wife	_____		_____
Total	$_____		$_____
____ years (est.) of retirement	×_____ Factor		×_____ Factor
Inflated Social Security	$_____		$_____
2. Pension	$_____		$_____
Inflation factor for ____ years of retirement (if pension rises with inflation)	×_____ Factor		×_____ Factor
Total pension	$_____		$_____
3. Other:			
a. Life insurance	$_____		$_____
b. Annuities			
i) Variable	$_____		$_____
ii) Fixed	$_____		$_____
c. Mutual funds	$_____		$_____
d. Thrift accounts	$_____		$_____
e. Stock dividends	$_____		$_____
f. Rents from real estate	$_____		$_____
g. Miscellaneous income	$_____		$_____
Total other income	$_____		$_____
4. Total income	$_____		$_____

Add all monthly sources of income. Be sure to inflate where it is possible. Enter on 4.

5. Estimated years of retirement
   ____ years × yearly estimated income =   _____
6. Add profit from sale of home. Take present value. $_____
   Inflation factor to years of retirement   ×_____
   Total   = $_____
7. Add 5 and 6.   = $_____
8. Total amount available $_____
9. Amount short:
   Enter line 16 from Form 1. $_____
   Subtract line 8, Form 2 $_____
   Amount of shortage, if any $_____

Suppose you come up $50,000 short and your estimated years of retirement are 20 years; then:

$$\frac{\$50,000}{20} = \$2,500 \text{ per year short}$$

This really is what must be planned for.

PENSION AND PROFIT-SHARING PLAN

Family member _____

Plan name _____

Name and address of employer _____
_____

Employer ID no. _____ Plan no. _____

Type of plan _____

Date joined _____ Date vested _____

Type of administration of plan _____

Plan administrator _____

Address _____ Telephone _____

Trustees (name and address) _____
_____
_____

Benefits _____
_____
_____

Other information _____
_____

PENSION AND PROFIT-SHARING PLAN

Family member _____

Plan name _____

Name and address of employer _____
_____

Employer ID no. _____ Plan no. _____

Type of plan _____

Date joined _____ Date vested _____

Type of administration of plan _____

Plan administrator _____

Address _____ Telephone _____

Trustees (name and address) _____
_____
_____

Benefits _____
_____
_____

Other information _____
_____

INCOME TAXES

Family Member	Year	Adjusted Gross Income	Refund or Balance Due (−,+)	Total Taxes Paid	Date Paid	Other Information
_____	____	_____	_____	_____	_____	_____
_____	____	_____	_____	_____	_____	_____
_____	____	_____	_____	_____	_____	_____
_____	____	_____	_____	_____	_____	_____
_____	____	_____	_____	_____	_____	_____
_____	____	_____	_____	_____	_____	_____
_____	____	_____	_____	_____	_____	_____
_____	____	_____	_____	_____	_____	_____
_____	____	_____	_____	_____	_____	_____
_____	____	_____	_____	_____	_____	_____
_____	____	_____	_____	_____	_____	_____
_____	____	_____	_____	_____	_____	_____
_____	____	_____	_____	_____	_____	_____
_____	____	_____	_____	_____	_____	_____
_____	____	_____	_____	_____	_____	_____
_____	____	_____	_____	_____	_____	_____
_____	____	_____	_____	_____	_____	_____

INCOME TAXES

Family Member	Year	Adjusted Gross Income	Refund or Balance Due (−,+)	Total Taxes Paid	Date Paid	Other Information

INVESTMENT ART, JEWELRY, AND ANTIQUES

YOUR TAX AND INSURANCE INVENTORY

Item	Description & Identification	Purchased Date/Price	Sold Date/Price	Other Information
____	____	____	____	____
____	____	____	____	____
____	____	____	____	____
____	____	____	____	____
____	____	____	____	____
____	____	____	____	____
____	____	____	____	____
____	____	____	____	____
____	____	____	____	____
____	____	____	____	____
____	____	____	____	____
____	____	____	____	____
____	____	____	____	____
____	____	____	____	____
____	____	____	____	____

INVESTMENT ART, JEWELRY, AND ANTIQUES

Item	Description & Identification	Purchased Date/Price	Sold Date/Price	Other Information

WILLS, TRUSTS, ESTATE PLANNING

HOW TO ESTIMATE THE SIZE OF YOUR ESTATE

Estate planning that saves money and minimizes problems after your death should begin with an inventory of your assets. The figures can be educated estimates. With the list your lawyer can intelligently advise you regarding gifts, trusts, and other devices that can reduce or eliminate estate and inheritance taxes. If your estate is changing in size, you may want to review your list periodically. Two additional model lists follow the one printed below.

Assets	Estimated Value	Ownership (Husband, Wife, Joint, in Trust for)	In Will? Yes No
Savings accounts	$ _____	_____	___ ___
Checking accounts	_____	_____	___ ___
U.S. savings bonds	_____	_____	___ ___
Money owed to you	_____	_____	___ ___
Art, jewelry, other personal property	_____	_____	___ ___
Automobiles	_____	_____	___ ___
Your home	_____	_____	___ ___
Other real estate	_____	_____	___ ___
Stocks	_____	_____	___ ___
Bonds	_____	_____	___ ___
Government securities	_____	_____	___ ___
Mutual funds	_____	_____	___ ___
Other investments	_____	_____	___ ___
Equity interest in your own business	_____	_____	___ ___

HOW TO ESTIMATE THE SIZE OF YOUR ESTATE (cont'd)

Assets	Estimated Value	Ownership (Husband, Wife, Joint, in Trust for)	In Will? Yes No
Individual life insurance	_____	_____	___ ___
Group life insurance	_____	_____	___ ___
Death benefits from pension or profit-sharing plans*	_____	_____	___ ___
Total	$_____	_____	___ ___

Liabilities**	Estimated Value
Current bills	$_____
Mortgage	_____
Auto loans	_____
Personal loans	_____
Installment loans	_____
Life insurance loans	_____
Income taxes	_____
Leases	_____
Other obligations	_____
Total	$_____

HOW TO ESTIMATE THE SIZE OF YOUR ESTATE (cont'd)

Total Value of Your Estate	Estimated Value
Assets minus liabilities	$_____
Deductions from Your Estate	
Burial expenses	$_____
Lawyer's fee	_____
Executor's fee	_____
Cost of liquidating assets	_____
Deduction for estate tax credit	_____
Marital deduction	_____
Orphan's exclusion	_____
Total	$_____
Total Taxable Estate	
Estate value minus deductions	$_____

*Not counting funds placed in IRA and Keogh plans and left to heirs.
**Excluding loans covered by credit life insurance.

HOW TO ESTIMATE THE SIZE OF YOUR ESTATE

Assets	Estimated Value	Ownership (Husband, Wife, Joint, in Trust for)	In Will? Yes	No
Savings accounts	$ _____	_____	___	___
Checking accounts	_____	_____	___	___
U.S. savings bonds	_____	_____	___	___
Money owed to you	_____	_____	___	___
Art, jewelry, other personal property	_____	_____	___	___
Automobiles	_____	_____	___	___
Your home	_____	_____	___	___
Other real estate	_____	_____	___	___
Stocks	_____	_____	___	___
Bonds	_____	_____	___	___
Government securities	_____	_____	___	___
Mutual funds	_____	_____	___	___
Other investments	_____	_____	___	___
Equity interest in your own business	_____	_____	___	___
Individual life insurance	_____	_____	___	___
Group life insurance	_____	_____	___	___
Death benefits from pension or profit-sharing plans*	_____	_____	___	___
Total	$ _____	_____	___	___

Liabilities**	Estimated Value
Current bills	$ _____
Mortgage	_____
Auto loans	_____
Personal loans	_____

HOW TO ESTIMATE THE SIZE OF YOUR ESTATE (cont'd)

Liabilities	Estimated Value
Installment loans	_____
Life insurance loans	_____
Income taxes	_____
Leases	_____
Other obligations	_____
Total	$_____

Total Value of Your Estate

Assets minus liabilities	$_____

Deductions from Your Estate

Burial expenses	$_____
Lawyer's fee	_____
Executor's fee	_____
Cost of liquidating assets	_____
Deduction for estate tax credit	_____
Marital deduction	_____
Orphan's exclusion	_____
Total	$_____

Total Taxable Estate

Estate value minus deductions	$_____

---

*Not counting funds placed in IRA and Keogh plans and left to heirs.
**Excluding loans covered by credit life insurance.

NET WORTH—ANNUAL CALCULATION

Your Financial Progress Reference

Assets	Year_____	Year_____	Year_____
Cash on hand	$_____	$_____	$_____
Savings accounts	_____	_____	_____
Checking accounts	_____	_____	_____
House, market value	_____	_____	_____
Other real estate, value	_____	_____	_____
Personal possessions, value	_____	_____	_____
Investment art & jewelry	_____	_____	_____
Automobile(s), blue book value	_____	_____	_____
Life insurance, cash value	_____	_____	_____
Stocks & bonds, today's value	_____	_____	_____
Mutual funds	_____	_____	_____
Contributions to pension funds	_____	_____	_____
Money owed you	_____	_____	_____
TOTAL	$_____	$_____	$_____

Obligations

Mortgages, balance due	$_____	$_____	$_____
Installment debts, balance due	_____	_____	_____
Credit cards, balance due	_____	_____	_____
Charge accounts, owed	_____	_____	_____
Other debts, total owed	_____	_____	_____
TOTAL	$_____	$_____	$_____
Net worth (assets minus obligations)	$_____	$_____	$_____

NET WORTH—ANNUAL CALCULATION (cont'd)

Year_____	Year_____	Year_____	Year_____	Year_____	Year_____
$_____	$_____	$_____	$_____	$_____	$_____
_____	_____	_____	_____	_____	_____
_____	_____	_____	_____	_____	_____
_____	_____	_____	_____	_____	_____
_____	_____	_____	_____	_____	_____
_____	_____	_____	_____	_____	_____
_____	_____	_____	_____	_____	_____
_____	_____	_____	_____	_____	_____
_____	_____	_____	_____	_____	_____
_____	_____	_____	_____	_____	_____
_____	_____	_____	_____	_____	_____
_____	_____	_____	_____	_____	_____
$_____	$_____	$_____	$_____	$_____	$_____
$_____	$_____	$_____	$_____	$_____	$_____
_____	_____	_____	_____	_____	_____
_____	_____	_____	_____	_____	_____
_____	_____	_____	_____	_____	_____
$_____	$_____	$_____	$_____	$_____	$_____
$_____	$_____	$_____	$_____	$_____	$_____

FORM FOR A SIMPLE WILL

LAST WILL AND TESTAMENT OF

_____

I, _____ , a resident of _____
(CITY)
_____ , _____ , make and publish this my last will and testament:
COUNTY   STATE
I hereby declare that I am _____ .
(SINGLE/MARRIED/DIVORCED)
The names of my children are _____ (if no children, it is advisable to list the names of your closest blood relatives).

I nominate _____ as executor/executrix of this my last will and tes-
(NAME OF PERSON)
tament. In the event my first choice cannot serve as executor, I nominate _____
_____ to serve as alternate executor. (Optional: I hereby authorize either my primary or secondary choice for executor to serve without bond.)

I leave the rest, residue and remainder of my estate to _____ . If he/she predeceases me or dies within ninety (90) days of my death, then I leave the rest, residue and remainder to _____ .

If my death leaves any of my minor children as orphans I nominate _____
_____ to serve as the guardian of the persons and estates of my minor children.

IN WITNESS WHEREOF, I have hereunto set my hand this ____ day of _____ , 19__, at _____ , _____ .
(CITY)   (STATE)

The foregoing instrument, entitled *Last Will and Testament,* was signed today by _____ in our joint presence, and at the same time, and we therefore sign as witnesses to the execution of this will. We declare under penalty of perjury that the foregoing is true and correct. Executed on this ____ day of _____ , 19__, at
_____ , _____ .
(CITY)   (STATE)

1. _____
   (WITNESS)
Residing at _____

2. _____
   (WITNESS)
Residing at _____

3. _____
   (WITNESS)
Residing at _____

WHAT EVERY HUSBAND AND WIFE SHOULD KNOW AFTER DRAWING UP WILLS

A Checklist

Life Insurance Policies

How many life insurance policies do you have? _____

Are all policies assembled in a convenient, safe, and readily accessible place—*not* your safe deposit box? _____

Have you a schedule of premium payments? _____

Are all premiums paid up-to-date? _____

Are there any outstanding loans against the policies? _____

Do you have a birth certificate kept with the policies (lack of proof of your age may cause some difficulty and an apparent misstatement of age may cause a reduction in the proceeds of the policy)? _____

Does your spouse know whom to call in the event of your death? _____

Does your spouse know what to do about filing proofs of claim for the policies? _____

Does your spouse know who can be of assistance in filing the proofs of claim? _____

Burial

Have you made burial plans? _____

Have you made these plans known to your spouse? _____

Have you and your spouse discussed the benefits which are available from Social Security, Veterans Administration, your employer, or any other source? _____

Regarding Your Wills

Do both of you know where the Wills are? _____

Does your spouse have a copy of your Will? _____

Are the Wills up-to-date? _____

Do they contain burial instructions or are the burial instructions separate? _____

Banks and Bank Accounts

At which banks do you maintain accounts? _____

Which are savings accounts and which are checking accounts? _____

Are all of the bank accounts joint and survivor accounts? _____

Is there at least one account in your spouse's name? _____

Where are the savings passbooks kept? _____

Are there papers for withdrawal by mail readily available and kept with each savings passbook? _____

WHAT EVERY HUSBAND AND WIFE SHOULD KNOW AFTER DRAWING UP WILLS (cont'd)

Safe Deposit Vaults

Do you have a safe deposit vault? _____

Where is it located? _____

Does your spouse know where it is? _____

Does your lawyer know where it is? _____

Is there a statement with your Will of the vault and vault number? _____

Where is the key? _____

Does your spouse have an extra key? _____

Does anyone have access? _____

What hours is the bank open? _____

Do you have a listing of papers in your safe deposit vault? _____

Emergency Funds

Will there be cash available, in the event of death, to pay the last expenses without strapping the family? _____

Will there be cash available to your spouse to pay living expenses for six months until your estate is settled? _____

Insurance Proceeds

How are the proceeds from your life insurance policies to be paid? _____

How much monthly income will your insurance furnish to your spouse and family? _____

For how long will this insurance be provided? _____

Is your spouse familiar with your estate plan and your intended deployment of assets? _____

Have you and your spouse considered a trust arrangement which names the other as a successor-trustee? _____

Is your spouse familiar with the insurance options? _____

Does your spouse understand about leaving the proceeds with the company? _____

Are the options irrevocable or subject to change as your children grow older? _____

Are your spouse's hands tied completely or is there leeway to exercise discretion and to provide for changing conditions? _____

Investments

Do you own any stocks? _____

Where are the stock certificates? _____

WHAT EVERY HUSBAND AND WIFE SHOULD KNOW AFTER DRAWING UP WILLS (cont'd)

Where are your bonds? _____

Are the stocks listed along with their dividend dates? _____

Where are the dividend checks mailed? _____

Are your securities fully paid for or is there a margin account? _____

If there is a margin account, is there a safe balance so there will not be any calls? _____

In the event of calls, which stocks would you want to sell and which to hold? _____

Are your stocks being used as collateral for any outstanding loans? _____

If you have any outstanding loans, are they covered by life insurance? _____

Business

Are you in business for yourself or with others? _____

What percentage of the business do you own? _____

Is there a written agreement with your associates or key employees to buy out your interest at a fair price if something happens to you? _____

Is there business insurance to cover your interest in the firm? _____

If there is a buy and sell agreement, is the agreement properly funded so your family can be compensated without endangering the business? _____

Is there any mortgage insurance? _____

Children and Grandchildren

Have you provided first for your spouse and then for your children? _____

Have you made realistic arrangements for your minor children? _____

Have you made arrangements for your children who have reached adulthood at the time of your death? _____

Have you left your spouse at least the minimum amount required by the law of your state? _____

Have you protected your children against invasion of their interests? _____

TRUST FUNDS

Established for	Date	Lawyer/Bank/Trustees	Location of Trust Agreement
_____	_____	_____	_____
_____	_____	_____	_____
_____	_____	_____	_____
_____	_____	_____	_____
_____	_____	_____	_____
_____	_____	_____	_____
_____	_____	_____	_____
_____	_____	_____	_____
_____	_____	_____	_____
_____	_____	_____	_____
_____	_____	_____	_____
_____	_____	_____	_____
_____	_____	_____	_____
_____	_____	_____	_____
_____	_____	_____	_____
_____	_____	_____	_____

GIFTS, BEQUESTS, AND WILLS

Family member _____ Date _____

Document _____

Prepared by _____

Witnesses _____

Location of document _____

Location of duplicate copies _____

Codicils/appendices _____

_____

Executors/executrixes _____

Bequests/trusts _____

If revised/destroyed, date _____

Family member _____ Date _____

Document _____

Prepared by _____

Witnesses _____

Location of document _____

Location of duplicate copies _____

Codicils/appendices _____

_____

Executors/executrixes _____

Bequests/trusts _____

If revised/destroyed, date _____

GIFTS, BEQUESTS, AND WILLS

Family member _____ Date _____

Document _____

Prepared by _____

Witnesses _____

Location of document _____

Location of duplicate copies _____

Codicils/appendices _____

_____

Executors/executrixes _____

Bequests/trusts _____

If revised/destroyed, date _____

Family member _____ Date _____

Document _____

Prepared by _____

Witnesses _____

Location of document _____

Location of duplicate copies _____

Codicils/appendices _____

_____

Executors/executrixes _____

Bequests/trusts _____

If revised/destroyed, date _____

LAST WILL AND TESTAMENT LOCATOR

WILL

Name _____ Dated _____

Attorney's name and address _____

_____

_____

Location of original _____

Location of copy _____

Executor's name and address _____

_____

Guardian's name and address _____

_____

Testamentary trust trustee's name and address _____

_____

If Will destroyed, date and method of destruction _____

_____

LAST WILL AND TESTAMENT LOCATOR (cont'd)

CODICILS

Dated _____ Location _____

Dated _____ Location _____

Dated _____ Location _____

Dated _____ Location _____

DEED OF TRUST

Dated _____

Trustee's name and address _____
_____

Beneficiaries _____
_____
_____
_____
_____

Corpus of trust _____

Location _____

LAST WILL AND TESTAMENT LOCATOR

WILL

Name _____ Dated _____

Attorney's name and address _____

_____

_____

Location of original _____

Location of copy _____

Executor's name and address _____

_____

Guardian's name and address _____

_____

Testamentary trust trustee's name and address _____

_____

If Will destroyed, date and method of destruction _____

_____

LAST WILL AND TESTAMENT LOCATOR (cont'd)

CODICILS

Dated _____ Location _____

Dated _____ Location _____

Dated _____ Location _____

Dated _____ Location _____

DEED OF TRUST

Dated _____

Trustee's name and address _____

_____

Beneficiaries _____

_____

_____

_____

_____

Corpus of trust _____

Location _____

THE ESTATE PLANNING TEAM

Estate of _____

Attorney

_____

_____

_____

Accountant

_____

_____

_____

Insurance advisor

_____

_____

_____

Bank or trust officer

_____

_____

_____

Remarks _____

_____

_____

_____

_____

THE ESTATE PLANNING TEAM

Estate of _____

Attorney

_____
_____
_____
_____

Accountant

_____
_____
_____
_____

Insurance advisor

_____
_____
_____
_____

Bank or trust officer

_____
_____
_____
_____

Remarks _____

_____
_____
_____
_____
_____

REPORTABLE GIFTS AND DONATIONS

Made by _____

Date _____ Recipient _____

Gift _____ Value _____

Made by _____

Date _____ Recipient _____

Gift _____ Value _____

Made by _____

Date _____ Recipient _____

Gift _____ Value _____

Made by _____

Date _____ Recipient _____

Gift _____ Value _____

Made by _____

Date _____ Recipient _____

Gift _____ Value _____

Made by _____

Date _____ Recipient _____

Gift _____ Value _____

Made by _____

Date _____ Recipient _____

Gift _____ Value _____

CURRENT CREDITORS

Date _____ Name _____ Amount _____

Reason _____

If paid, location of discharge papers _____

Location of supporting documents _____

Date _____ Name _____ Amount _____

Reason _____

If paid, location of discharge papers _____

Location of supporting documents _____

Date _____ Name _____ Amount _____

Reason _____

If paid, location of discharge papers _____

Location of supporting documents _____

Date _____ Name _____ Amount _____

Reason _____

If paid, location of discharge papers _____

Location of supporting documents _____

Date _____ Name _____ Amount _____

Reason _____

If paid, location of discharge papers _____

Location of supporting documents _____

Date _____ Name _____ Amount _____

Reason _____

If paid, location of discharge papers _____

Location of supporting documents _____

CURRENT DEBTORS

Date _____ Name _____ Amount _____

Reason _____

Security, if any _____

Location of supporting documents _____

Date _____ Name _____ Amount _____

Reason _____

Security, if any _____

Location of supporting documents _____

Date _____ Name _____ Amount _____

Reason _____

Security, if any _____

Location of supporting documents _____

Date _____ Name _____ Amount _____

Reason _____

Security, if any _____

Location of supporting documents _____

Date _____ Name _____ Amount _____

Reason _____

Security, if any _____

Location of supporting documents _____

TRUST PROPERTY RECORD

Nature of property _____

Location _____

Settlor _____

Amount/value _____ Date _____

Beneficiary _____

Kind of trust _____

Conditions of trust _____

_____

_____

_____

_____

Nature of property _____

Location _____

Settlor _____

Amount/value _____ Date _____

Beneficiary _____

Kind of trust _____

Conditions of trust _____

_____

_____

_____

_____

OTHER INVESTMENTS

Kind	Date Purch.	Cost	Owned by	Date Sold	Price
_____	_____	_____	_____	_____	_____
_____	_____	_____	_____	_____	_____
_____	_____	_____	_____	_____	_____
_____	_____	_____	_____	_____	_____
_____	_____	_____	_____	_____	_____
_____	_____	_____	_____	_____	_____
_____	_____	_____	_____	_____	_____
_____	_____	_____	_____	_____	_____
_____	_____	_____	_____	_____	_____
_____	_____	_____	_____	_____	_____
_____	_____	_____	_____	_____	_____
_____	_____	_____	_____	_____	_____
_____	_____	_____	_____	_____	_____
_____	_____	_____	_____	_____	_____
_____	_____	_____	_____	_____	_____

RENTAL PROPERTY

Address _____

Owner/landlord _____

Date (from-to) _____ Rental price _____

Address _____

Owner/landlord _____

Date (from-to) _____ Rental price _____

Address _____

Owner/landlord _____

Date (from-to) _____ Rental price _____

Address _____

Owner/landlord _____

Date (from-to) _____ Rental price _____

Address _____

Owner/landlord _____

Date (from-to) _____ Rental price _____

Address _____

Owner/landlord _____

Date (from-to) _____ Rental price _____

MOTOR VEHICLES

Make _____ Year _____ Model _____

Purchased from _____

Date of purchase _____ Price _____ ID/VIN no. _____

Sales/trade date _____ Price _____ Mileage _____

Purchased by _____

Make _____ Year _____ Model _____

Purchased from _____

Date of purchase _____ Price _____ ID/VIN no. _____

Sales/trade date _____ Price _____ Mileage _____

Purchased by _____

Make _____ Year _____ Model _____

Purchased from _____

Date of purchase _____ Price _____ ID/VIN no. _____

Sales/trade date _____ Price _____ Mileage _____

Purchased by _____

Make _____ Year _____ Model _____

Purchased from _____

Date of purchase _____ Price _____ ID/VIN no. _____

Sales/trade date _____ Price _____ Mileage _____

Purchased by _____

NOTHING IS CERTAIN . . .

LAST RITES INFORMATION

Family member _____

Date of death _____ Place _____

Burial _____   Entombment _____   Inurnment _____

Held on (date) _____ Where _____

_____

Family member _____

Date of death _____ Place _____

Burial _____   Entombment _____   Inurnment _____

Held on (date) _____ Where _____

_____

Family member _____

Date of death _____ Place _____

Burial _____   Entombment _____   Inurnment _____

Held on (date) _____ Where _____

_____

Family member _____

Date of death _____ Place _____

Burial _____   Entombment _____   Inurnment _____

Held on (date) _____ Where _____

_____

LAST RITES INFORMATION

Family member _____

Date of death _____ Place _____

Burial _____ Entombment _____ Inurnment _____

Held on (date) _____ Where _____

_____

Family member _____

Date of death _____ Place _____

Burial _____ Entombment _____ Inurnment _____

Held on (date) _____ Where _____

_____

Family member _____

Date of death _____ Place _____

Burial _____ Entombment _____ Inurnment _____

Held on (date) _____ Where _____

_____

Family member _____

Date of death _____ Place _____

Burial _____ Entombment _____ Inurnment _____

Held on (date) _____ Where _____

_____

INFORMATION IN THE EVENT OF DEATH

Name _____

SOCIAL SECURITY

Social Security no. _____

Location of Social Security card _____
_____

Location of employment record showing Social Security payments _____
_____
_____

MILITARY SERVICE

I am ____ am not ____ a veteran of the U.S. Armed Forces.

Active duty from _____ to _____

Branch _____ Rank _____

Service serial no. _____

Location of military papers _____

AVAILABILITY OF IMMEDIATE CASH

Lump sum insurance _____

Company or companies _____
_____

Lump sum Social Security _____

Other money available _____
_____

INFORMATION IN THE EVENT OF DEATH (cont'd)

REQUESTED FUNERAL ARRANGEMENTS

Religious preference _____

I would _____ would not _____ like full military honors.

I would _____ would not _____ like a fraternal funeral.

Remarks _____

Funeral director _____

Address _____ Telephone _____

Burial information:

Cemetery _____ Address _____

I wish to be buried _____ cremated _____ entombed _____

Burial contract date _____ Cremation contract date _____

I do _____ do not _____ have a niche or lot.

Location _____ Lot purchase date _____

PERPETUAL CARE

Amount paid $ _____ Date _____

Special services desired _____

_____

I would prefer flowers _____ contributions to charity _____

Name of charity _____

Address _____

Request undertaker to provide _____ copies of my death certificate. (Copies will be needed by each life insurance company, for real estate title transfer, government benefits, Social Security and VA, personal property and securities, stocks/bonds, vehicle registrations, etc.)

INFORMATION IN THE EVENT OF DEATH (cont'd)

PERSONS TO BE NOTIFIED IN CASE OF DEATH

Name _____ Telephone _____

Address _____

Name _____ Telephone _____

Address _____

Name _____ Telephone _____

Address _____

Additional addresses in my address book, located at
_____

POST-MORTEM POWER OF ATTORNEY

Name _____ General or special _____

Location of documents _____

Dated _____ Revoked _____

Name _____ General or special _____

Location of documents _____

Dated _____ Revoked _____

INFORMATION IN THE EVENT OF DEATH

Name _____

SOCIAL SECURITY

Social Security no. _____

Location of Social Security card _____
_____

Location of employment record showing Social Security payments _____
_____
_____

MILITARY SERVICE

I am ____ am not ____ a veteran of the U.S. Armed Forces.

Active duty from _____ to _____

Branch _____ Rank _____

Service serial no. _____

Location of military papers _____

AVAILABILITY OF IMMEDIATE CASH

Lump sum insurance _____

Company or companies _____
_____

Lump sum Social Security _____

Other money available _____
_____

INFORMATION IN THE EVENT OF DEATH (cont'd)

REQUESTED FUNERAL ARRANGEMENTS

Religious preference _____

I would ____   would not ____   like full military honors.

I would ____   would not ____   like a fraternal funeral.

Remarks _____

Funeral director _____

Address _____ Telephone _____

Burial information:

Cemetery _____ Address _____

I wish to be buried ____   cremated ____   entombed ____

Burial contract date _____ Cremation contract date _____

I do ____   do not ____   have a niche or lot.

Location _____ Lot purchase date _____

PERPETUAL CARE

Amount paid $ _____ Date _____

Special services desired _____

_____

I would prefer flowers ____   contributions to charity ____

Name of charity _____

Address _____

Request undertaker to provide ____ copies of my death certificate. (Copies will be needed by each life insurance company, for real estate title transfer, government benefits, Social Security and VA, personal property and securities, stocks/bonds, vehicle registrations, etc.)

INFORMATION IN THE EVENT OF DEATH (cont'd)

PERSONS TO BE NOTIFIED IN CASE OF DEATH

Name _____ Telephone _____

Address _____

Name _____ Telephone _____

Address _____

Name _____ Telephone _____

Address _____

Additional addresses in my address book, located at
_____

POST-MORTEM POWER OF ATTORNEY

Name _____ General or special _____

Location of documents _____

Dated _____ Revoked _____

Name _____ General or special _____

Location of documents _____

Dated _____ Revoked _____

CHECKLIST—STEPS TO TAKE AFTER A FAMILY LOSS

- ____ Delegate as many tasks as possible to relatives and friends:
    - —Notifying other relatives, fellow employees, out-of-towners
    - —Answering telephone and keeping record of callers
    - —Looking after young children and preparing meals
- ____ Discuss arrangements with funeral director
- ____ Obtain several copies of death certificate
- ____ Arrange to see lawyer and executor and start probate of Will
- ____ Review death benefit claims and file for same:
    - —Social Security
    - —Life insurance
    - —Veterans benefits
    - —Labor union benefits
    - —Fraternal or social or professional organization benefits
    - —Employer benefits
- ____ Contact family banker/broker/accountant
- ____ Obtain claim forms from life insurance companies
- ____ Notify insurer carrying deceased's homeowners and auto insurance policies
- ____ Notify personnel department where deceased was employed
- ____ Destroy credit cards
- ____ Suspend any open orders with stock broker
- ____ Search for assets and liabilities and determine location of data
    - —Policies, passbooks, real estate deeds, check books
    - —Tax returns, auto registrations, loans and payment books
    - —Safe deposit boxes, credit insurance, mortgage insurance
- ____ Open estate checking account
- ____ Pay bills owing by decedent
- ____ Obtain trusted counsel and advice for safekeeping and investment of assets
- ____ Arrange for proper distribution of assets to rightful heirs
- ____ Carefully consider before making any gifts at this time
- ____ File appropriate tax and estate returns
- ____ Send note of appreciation to all who attended and assisted

CHECKLIST FOR MY EXECUTOR

REQUESTS AND SUGGESTIONS

People who should be notified of my death _____

_____

Arrangements I would like made for my body _____

_____

Funeral and cemetery plans _____

_____

My signed will is on file at _____

My intention is to have my will probated in the state of _____

The location of my important records, including birth certificate, information on taxes, military service, and any previous marriages _____

_____

_____

My Social Security number is _____

I suggest that the following professionals be retained to help you manage my estate

_____

_____

_____

My minor children should be cared for by _____

_____

Information for newspaper obituaries can be obtained from _____

_____

Additional suggestions _____

_____

_____

FAMILY ADVISERS WHO HAVE ADDITIONAL RECORDS

	Name	**Address**
Lawyer	_____	_____
Accountant	_____	_____
Banker	_____	_____
Broker	_____	_____
Insurance agent	_____	_____
Doctor	_____	_____

CHECKLIST FOR MY EXECUTOR (cont'd)

LOCATION OF ASSETS

Safe deposit boxes _____

Checking accounts _____

Savings accounts _____

Savings bonds _____

Securities _____

Retirement and
death benefit information _____

Life insurance policies _____

Credit union _____

Debts receivable _____

Valuable collections _____

Information on royalties,
claims, and legacies _____

CHECKLIST OF CHORES

____ See that funeral arrangements are made.

____ Choose an attorney.

____ Discuss estate affairs with him, including the best way to collect and preserve assets. Set his fee.

____ Have the attorney start probate proceedings.

____ After you have been officially appointed executor, ask the lawyer for a letter describing your responsibilities and outlining what arrangements he will make to conduct the normal business of the estate, such as notifying those with a legal interest, paying for funeral expenses, and allotting for immediate family needs.

____ Inventory the assets and documents of the estate. Plan whether to carry on or liquidate investments or a business if the will gives no specific instructions.

____ Hire accountants or investment advisers if needed.

____ Discuss with the lawyer the best timetable for payment of all taxes and check to see they are prepared and paid as due.

____ After the will is probated, approve payment of the valid debts of the estate.

____ Arrange the distribution of cash legacies specified in the will. Account to the appropriate court if required and make the final distribution to the beneficiaries of the balance of the estate.

CHECKLIST FOR MY EXECUTOR (cont'd)

SURVIVORS

(Parents, spouse, natural and adopted children, siblings, or others)

Name	Address	Relationship
_____	_____	_____
_____	_____	_____
_____	_____	_____
_____	_____	_____
_____	_____	_____
_____	_____	_____
_____	_____	_____
_____	_____	_____
_____	_____	_____
_____	_____	_____

ESTIMATED NET WORTH

Value of major assets _____ minus value of liabilities _____

equals net worth _____.

LIABILITIES

Mortgages _____

Installment loans_____

_____

Other major debts _____

_____

Lawsuits pending _____

_____

Taxes _____

_____

Signed_____

Date_____

CHECKLIST FOR MY EXECUTOR

REQUESTS AND SUGGESTIONS

People who should be notified of my death _____

_____

Arrangements I would like made for my body _____

_____

Funeral and cemetery plans _____

_____

My signed will is on file at _____

My intention is to have my will probated in the state of _____

The location of my important records, including birth certificate, information on taxes, military service, and any previous marriages _____

_____

_____

My Social Security number is _____

I suggest that the following professionals be retained to help you manage my estate

_____

_____

_____

My minor children should be cared for by _____

_____

Information for newspaper obituaries can be obtained from _____

_____

Additional suggestions _____

_____

_____

FAMILY ADVISERS WHO HAVE ADDITIONAL RECORDS

	Name	**Address**
Lawyer	_____	_____
Accountant	_____	_____
Banker	_____	_____
Broker	_____	_____
Insurance agent	_____	_____
Doctor	_____	_____

CHECKLIST FOR MY EXECUTOR (cont'd)

LOCATION OF ASSETS

Safe deposit boxes _____

Checking accounts _____

Savings accounts _____

Savings bonds _____

Securities _____

Retirement and
death benefit information _____

Life insurance policies _____

Credit union _____

Debts receivable _____

Valuable collections _____

Information on royalties,
claims, and legacies _____

CHECKLIST OF CHORES

___ See that funeral arrangements are made.

___ Choose an attorney.

___ Discuss estate affairs with him, including the best way to collect and preserve assets. Set his fee.

___ Have the attorney start probate proceedings.

___ After you have been officially appointed executor, ask the lawyer for a letter describing your responsibilities and outlining what arrangements he will make to conduct the normal business of the estate, such as notifying those with a legal interest, paying for funeral expenses, and allotting for immediate family needs.

___ Inventory the assets and documents of the estate. Plan whether to carry on or liquidate investments or a business if the will gives no specific instructions.

___ Hire accountants or investment advisers if needed.

___ Discuss with the lawyer the best timetable for payment of all taxes and check to see they are prepared and paid as due.

___ After the will is probated, approve payment of the valid debts of the estate.

___ Arrange the distribution of cash legacies specified in the will. Account to the appropriate court if required and make the final distribution to the beneficiaries of the balance of the estate.

CHECKLIST FOR MY EXECUTOR (cont'd)

SURVIVORS

(Parents, spouse, natural and adopted children, siblings, or others)

Name	Address	Relationship
_____	_____	_____
_____	_____	_____
_____	_____	_____
_____	_____	_____
_____	_____	_____
_____	_____	_____
_____	_____	_____
_____	_____	_____
_____	_____	_____

ESTIMATED NET WORTH

Value of major assets _____ minus value of liabilities _____

equals net worth _____.

LIABILITIES

Mortgages _____

Installment loans_____

_____

Other major debts _____

_____

Lawsuits pending _____

_____

Taxes _____

_____

Signed _____

Date _____

UNIFORM DONOR CARD ("ANATOMICAL GIFT")

UNIFORM DONOR CARD

OF _____
(Print or type name of donor)

In the hope that I may help others, I hereby make this anatomical gift, if medically acceptable, to take effect on my death. The words and marks below indicate my desires.

I give: (a)____any needed organs or parts

           (b)____only the following organs or parts

_____
(Specify the organ(s) or part(s))

for the purposes of transplantation, therapy, medical research, or education;

           (c)____my body for anatomical study if needed.

Limitations or
special wishes, if any: _____

Signed by the donor and the following two witnesses in the presence of each other:

Signature of donor	Date of birth of donor
Date signed	City and state
Witness	Witness

(This is a legal document under the Uniform Anatomical Gift Act or similar laws.)

PART IV

YOUR MONEY, YOUR RESUME, GOING INTO BUSINESS, MISCELLANY

YOUR MONEY, YOUR RESUME, GOING INTO BUSINESS, MISCELLANY

Money matters.

It matters to everyone, but in different ways. To some, money may mean economic independence. To others, it may suggest a Pandora's Box of unsolvable problems. To still others, it may represent status, power, prestige.

However it matters to you, forms, records, and checklists offer methods of keeping both track and control of business and family economic affairs. The records you generate in key areas obviously become necessary at income tax and similar times. But the records you keep with the aid of this book should have a more long-range purpose. They should, for example, give you a synoptic view of how you've been doing, where you are going, at what rate, and what you should watch for.

Your records should also help you reduce the risks that each of us takes when he goes job-hunting or into business. The risks center on nearly everyone's need to change course at some point in his or her life: to switch companies, to find a first job, to start a new enterprise.

Money and related decisions give some people the willies. Rational thinking may stop. Sweat may break out. Grey hairs may multiply. But even those who face money decisions with a calm mind need numbers for support when the Moment of Economic Truth arrives.

The following are some basic forms that will, when used with other records in this book, help you prepare.

SHOPPING FOR A BANK?
ASK (AT LEAST) THESE QUESTIONS

- Is there a minimum required balance on regular checking accounts?
- What about a service charge for checks?
- Are there extra charges on other bank services such as safe deposit boxes?
- What about the availability of installment loans? At what interest rate?
- What about the availability and terms of mortgages?
- What types of investment/savings plans are offered?
- What are the rates of interest on different accounts and how often are they compounded and credited?
- Are there any restrictions on withdrawing your money?
- Are your deposits federally or state insured?
- What about special checking accounts (no minimum balance)?

THE RESUME: SOME THINGS TO INCLUDE

_____ YOUR NAME

_____ YOUR ADDRESS

_____ TELEPHONE NUMBER

_____ YOUR CAREER OBJECTIVES: What you want to be when you grow up, so to speak.

_____ POSITION DESIRED: Or applied for.

_____ SALARY REQUIREMENT: It is best to put "negotiable," but if you must have a minimum monthly income, do not be afraid to say so.

_____ PROFESSIONAL QUALIFICATIONS: Where you have worked and in what position, but not details—they can go in your job application; a resume should not look like a job history, only job highlights.

_____ BUSINESS HISTORY: Include if you've worked for yourself.

_____ EDUCATION: Where you went to school; degrees earned.

_____ HONORS, AWARDS, OFFICES: It may seem odd to include the fact that you were Miss Congeniality in 1966, but this gives a bit of a picture of you; and if you happen to be applying for a position that involves dealing with people, being Miss Congeniality may be important.

_____ MILITARY SERVICE

_____ SPORTS, OUTSIDE INTERESTS, HOBBIES: This is to let prospective employers know something about you, the person.

_____ TRAVEL: Major trips, assignments.

_____ REFERENCES: You can either list two or three nonrelatives or put "Available upon request," which is often preferred and saves space.

_____ SPECIAL QUALIFICATIONS: Speak eighteen languages fluently, can drive a limousine, available on weekends—any information that makes you a little different from someone else.

EMPLOYMENT HISTORY

Family member _____

Employer _____ Position held _____

Address _____

Telephone no. _____ Supervisor _____

References _____

Promoted to _____ Date _____

Responsibilities _____

_____

Date began _____ Date left _____

Starting salary _____ Ending salary _____

Reason for leaving _____

Family member _____

Employer _____ Position held _____

Address _____

Telephone no. _____ Supervisor _____

References _____

Promoted to _____ Date _____

Responsibilities _____

_____

Date began _____ Date left _____

Starting salary _____ Ending salary _____

Reason for leaving _____

EMPLOYMENT HISTORY

Family member _____

Employer _____ Position held _____

Address _____

Telephone no. _____ Supervisor _____

References _____

Promoted to _____ Date _____

Responsibilities _____

_____

Date began _____ Date left _____

Starting salary _____ Ending salary _____

Reason for leaving _____

Family member _____

Employer _____ Position held _____

Address _____

Telephone no. _____ Supervisor _____

References _____

Promoted to _____ Date _____

Responsibilities _____

_____

Date began _____ Date left _____

Starting salary _____ Ending salary _____

Reason for leaving _____

EMPLOYMENT HISTORY

Family member _____

Employer _____ Position held _____

Address _____

Telephone no. _____ Supervisor _____

References _____

Promoted to _____ Date _____

Responsibilities _____

_____

Date began _____ Date left _____

Starting salary _____ Ending salary _____

Reason for leaving _____

Family member _____

Employer _____ Position held _____

Address _____

Telephone no. _____ Supervisor _____

References _____

Promoted to _____ Date _____

Responsibilities _____

_____

Date began _____ Date left _____

Starting salary _____ Ending salary _____

Reason for leaving _____

EMPLOYMENT HISTORY

Family member _____

Employer _____ Position held _____

Address _____

Telephone no. _____ Supervisor _____

References _____

Promoted to _____ Date _____

Responsibilities _____
_____

Date began _____ Date left _____

Starting salary _____ Ending salary _____

Reason for leaving _____

Family member _____

Employer _____ Position held _____

Address _____

Telephone no. _____ Supervisor _____

References _____

Promoted to _____ Date _____

Responsibilities _____
_____

Date began _____ Date left _____

Starting salary _____ Ending salary _____

Reason for leaving _____

EDUCATION

Family member _____ Dates attended _____

Name of school _____

Address _____ Telephone _____

Degree _____ Major _____

Awards/honors/prizes/achievements _____

_____

_____

_____

_____

Recommendations and references _____

_____

_____

_____

_____

Extracurricular activities or sports _____

_____

_____

_____

_____

Names to remember _____

_____

_____

_____

_____

EDUCATION

Family member _____ Dates attended _____

Name of school _____

Address _____ Telephone _____

Degree _____ Major _____

Awards/honors/prizes/achievements _____

_____

_____

_____

_____

Recommendations and references _____

_____

_____

_____

_____

_____

Extracurricular activities or sports _____

_____

_____

_____

_____

Names to remember _____

_____

_____

_____

_____

EDUCATION

Family member _____ Dates attended _____

Name of school _____

Address _____ Telephone _____

Degree _____ Major _____

Awards/honors/prizes/achievements _____

_____

_____

_____

_____

Recommendations and references _____

_____

_____

_____

_____

Extracurricular activities or sports _____

_____

_____

_____

_____

Names to remember _____

_____

_____

_____

_____

EDUCATION

Family member _____ Dates attended _____

Name of school _____

Address _____ Telephone _____

Degree _____ Major _____

Awards/honors/prizes/achievements _____

_____

_____

_____

_____

Recommendations and references _____

_____

_____

_____

_____

Extracurricular activities or sports _____

_____

_____

_____

Names to remember _____

_____

_____

_____

_____

EDUCATION

Family member _____ Dates attended _____

Name of school _____

Address _____ Telephone _____

Degree _____ Major _____

Awards/honors/prizes/achievements _____
_____
_____
_____
_____

Recommendations and references _____
_____
_____
_____
_____

Extracurricular activities or sports _____
_____
_____
_____
_____

Names to remember _____
_____
_____
_____
_____

EDUCATION

Family member _____ Dates attended _____

Name of school _____

Address _____ Telephone _____

Degree _____ Major _____

Awards/honors/prizes/achievements _____

_____

_____

_____

_____

Recommendations and references _____

_____

_____

_____

_____

Extracurricular activities or sports _____

_____

_____

_____

_____

Names to remember _____

_____

_____

_____

_____

BUSINESS HISTORY

Family member _____

Name of business _____

Address _____ Telephone _____

Type of business _____

Date started _____ Date closed/sold _____

Your participation _____

Bank _____ Banker _____

Account no(s). _____ Telephone _____

Attorney _____ Telephone _____

Accountant _____ Telephone _____

Names of partners/stockholders/employees _____

_____

_____

_____

Location of important documents and papers _____

_____

_____

Major suppliers _____

_____

_____

Major accounts _____

_____

_____

BUSINESS HISTORY

Family member _____

Name of business _____

Address _____ Telephone _____

Type of business _____

Date started _____ Date closed/sold _____

Your participation _____

Bank _____ Banker _____

Account no(s). _____ Telephone _____

Attorney _____ Telephone _____

Accountant _____ Telephone _____

Names of partners/stockholders/employees _____

_____

_____

_____

Location of important documents and papers _____

_____

_____

Major suppliers _____

_____

_____

Major accounts _____

_____

_____

MEMBERSHIPS IN ORGANIZATIONS—
WITH OFFICES, HONORS, AWARDS

Record all social, fraternal, and professional groups to which you belong.

Family member _____

Name of organization _____

Address _____

Dates (from-to) _____

Offices, honors, awards _____

_____

Family member _____

Name of organization _____

Address _____

Dates (from-to) _____

Offices, honors, awards _____

_____

Family member _____

Name of organization _____

Address _____

Dates (from-to) _____

Offices, honors, awards _____

_____

Family member _____

Name of organization _____

Address _____

Dates (from-to) _____

Offices, honors, awards _____

_____

MEMBERSHIPS IN ORGANIZATIONS—
WITH OFFICES, HONORS, AWARDS

Record all social, fraternal, and professional groups to which you belong.

Family member _____

Name of organization _____

Address _____

Dates (from-to) _____

Offices, honors, awards _____

_____

Family member _____

Name of organization _____

Address _____

Dates (from-to) _____

Offices, honors, awards _____

_____

Family member _____

Name of organization _____

Address _____

Dates (from-to) _____

Offices, honors, awards _____

_____

Family member _____

Name of organization _____

Address _____

Dates (from-to) _____

Offices, honors, awards _____

_____

MILITARY SERVICE

Family member _____ Service no. _____

Date enlisted or inducted _____ Service _____

Job classification _____

Training camps _____

Schools attended _____

_____

_____

ORGANIZATIONS:

    Company _____ Division _____

    Regiment _____ Dept. or ship _____

Transfers _____

Promotions and dates _____

_____

Citations _____

_____

Commanding officers _____

Overseas service _____

_____

Combat duty _____

_____

Important leaves or furloughs _____

_____

Date of discharge or separation _____

Recorded at _____

MILITARY SERVICE

Family member _____ Service no. _____

Date enlisted or inducted _____ Service _____

Job classification _____

Training camps _____

Schools attended _____

_____

_____

ORGANIZATIONS:

    Company _____ Division _____

    Regiment _____ Dept. or ship _____

Transfers _____

Promotions and dates _____

_____

Citations _____

_____

Commanding officers _____

Overseas service _____

_____

Combat duty _____

_____

Important leaves or furloughs _____

_____

Date of discharge or separation _____

Recorded at _____

SPORTS, OUTSIDE INTERESTS, HOBBIES

Family member _____

Interest, Hobby, and Name of Team and/or Place Played	Dates	Tournaments, Awards, Teammates, Coaches, Other Facts

SPORTS, OUTSIDE INTERESTS, HOBBIES

Family member _____

Interest, Hobby, and Name of Team and/or Place Played	Dates	Tournaments, Awards, Teammates, Coaches, Other Facts

SPORTS, OUTSIDE INTERESTS, HOBBIES

Family member _____

Interest, Hobby, and Name of Team and/or Place Played	Dates	Tournaments, Awards, Teammates, Coaches, Other Facts

SPORTS, OUTSIDE INTERESTS, HOBBIES

Family member _____

Interest, Hobby, and Name of Team and/or Place Played	Dates	Tournaments, Awards, Teammates, Coaches, Other Facts

SPORTS, OUTSIDE INTERESTS, HOBBIES

Family member _____

Interest, Hobby, and Name of Team and/or Place Played	Dates	Tournaments, Awards, Teammates, Coaches, Other Facts
_____	_____	_____
_____	_____	_____
_____	_____	_____
_____	_____	_____
_____	_____	_____
_____	_____	_____
_____	_____	_____
_____	_____	_____
_____	_____	_____
_____	_____	_____
_____	_____	_____
_____	_____	_____
_____	_____	_____
_____	_____	_____

SPORTS, OUTSIDE INTERESTS, HOBBIES

Family member _____

Interest, Hobby, and Name of Team and/or Place Played	Dates	Tournaments, Awards, Teammates, Coaches, Other Facts

TRAVEL

Family member(s) _____ Dates _____

Places visited _____

_____

Travel companions _____

Purpose _____

Travel for or arranged by _____

Family member(s) _____ Dates _____

Places visited _____

_____

Travel companions _____

Purpose _____

Travel for or arranged by _____

Family member(s) _____ Dates _____

Places visited _____

_____

Travel companions _____

Purpose _____

Travel for or arranged by _____

Family member(s) _____ Dates _____

Places visited _____

_____

Travel companions _____

Purpose _____

Travel for or arranged by _____

TRAVEL

Family member(s) _____ Dates _____

Places visited _____

_____

Travel companions _____

Purpose _____

Travel for or arranged by _____

Family member(s) _____ Dates _____

Places visited _____

_____

Travel companions _____

Purpose _____

Travel for or arranged by _____

Family member(s) _____ Dates _____

Places visited _____

_____

Travel companions _____

Purpose _____

Travel for or arranged by _____

Family member(s) _____ Dates _____

Places visited _____

_____

Travel companions _____

Purpose _____

Travel for or arranged by _____

A CHECKLIST ON FRANCHISES

_____ How long has the parent firm been in business?

_____ What is its financial strength?

_____ What are the background and experience of the company officers?

_____ What is the source of the company's earnings? If they make their profits from selling products to franchisees or from royalties (instead of simply selling franchises), they are more likely to be interested in your staying in business.

_____ How well is the product selling? How well has it sold in the past? *Assess the product on its merits.*

_____ Is your sales territory well-defined and exclusive?

_____ What is the level of competition in your sales area?

_____ Does the franchisor provide continuing assistance?

_____ What kind and through whom?

_____ Is training offered for franchisees and key employees?

_____ How and where is the product advertised? What will be your share of advertising costs?

_____ Examine the contract carefully. Does it cover all aspects of the agreement? Have your lawyer read it.

_____ Have you received the franchisor's disclosure statement, as required by law?

YOUR CAR AGAIN: CALCULATING PRESENT-CAR COSTS VERSUS NEW-CAR COSTS

	Present Costs	Proposed Costs
Fixed Charges:		
Depreciation (divide by number of years of ownership)	_____	_____
Insurance (yearly bill)	_____	_____
Finance charges or interest loss (divide by years of ownership)	_____	_____
Taxes and fees (divide sales tax and title fee by years of ownership, and license fee by number of years license is valid; add that one-year total to yearly total of property tax, registration, inspection)	_____	_____
Variable Charges:		
Gasoline and oil (yearly total)	_____	_____
Maintenance (yearly total, including tires, batteries, repairs)	_____	_____
Yearly total	_____	_____
Divide yearly total by yearly mileage	_____	_____
Cost per mile	_____	_____

THE FAMILY AUTOMOBILE:
YOUR INVESTMENT IN TRANSPORTATION

Owner/Driver	Make/Year/Model	Date Purch.	Purch. Price	Purch'd/Leased from	Ins. Agent: Add. & Phone	Auto Club, Other Memberships	Location of Papers	Date Sold	Price

PET RECORD

PURCHASE RECORD for _____

(name of Pet) _____

From: Name _____

          Address _____

Date _____ Contact _____

Telephone no. _____ Price _____

Breed _____

VITAL STATISTICS

Pedigreed name _____

Pedigreed description:

Born _____ Sex _____

Sire _____ Dam _____

Litter no. _____

AKC (pet) _____

AKC (dealer) _____

Papers sent _____ Papers received _____

HEALTH RECORD

Veterinarian _____

Address _____ Telephone _____

PET RECORD (cont'd)

Immunization record (dog):	Due	Given
(Temporary)		
Distemper	_____	_____
Hepatitis	_____	_____
Leptospirosis	_____	_____
(Adult)		
Distemper	_____	_____
Hepatitis	_____	_____
Leptospirosis	_____	_____
Rabies vaccination	_____	_____

(Yearly booster) 19__/ 19__/ 19__/ 19__/ 19__/ 19__/ 19__/ 19__/ 19__

  Rabies ___ ___ ___ ___ ___ ___ ___ ___ ___

  D-H-L ___ ___ ___ ___ ___ ___ ___ ___ ___

Immunization record (cat):	Due	Given
Feline pneumonitis	_____	_____
Booster	_____	_____
Feline distemper	_____	_____
Booster	_____	_____
Rabies vaccination	_____	_____

(Yearly booster) 19__/ 19__/ 19__/ 19__/ 19__/ 19__/ 19__/ 19__/ 19__

  Rabies ___ ___ ___ ___ ___ ___ ___ ___ ___

  D-H-L ___ ___ ___ ___ ___ ___ ___ ___ ___

AN AIDE-MEMOIRE—
IMPORTANT DATES TO REMEMBER

(Anniversaries, birthdays, due dates, financial income dates, special occasions, social, etc.)

| **Month of JANUARY** | | **Month of FEBRUARY** | |
Date	Occasion	Date	Occasion

AN AIDE-MEMOIRE—
IMPORTANT DATES TO REMEMBER (cont'd)

Month of MARCH		Month of APRIL	
Date	Occasion	Date	Occasion

AN AIDE-MEMOIRE—
IMPORTANT DATES TO REMEMBER (cont'd)

Month of MAY		Month of JUNE	
Date	Occasion	Date	Occasion

AN AIDE-MEMOIRE—
IMPORTANT DATES TO REMEMBER (cont'd)

Month of JULY		Month of AUGUST	
Date	Occasion	Date	Occasion

AN AIDE-MEMOIRE—
IMPORTANT DATES TO REMEMBER (cont'd)

Month of SEPTEMBER		Month of OCTOBER	
Date	Occasion	Date	Occasion

AN AIDE-MEMOIRE—
IMPORTANT DATES TO REMEMBER (cont'd)

Month of NOVEMBER		Month of DECEMBER	
Date	Occasion	Date	Occasion

Notes

Notes

Notes

Notes

Notes